T0359704

Negotiate YOUR Worth

SAM TRATTLES

First published in Australia in 2022
by KMD Books
Waikiki, WA 6169

Cover and interior design by Ida Jansson
Edited by Diane Hopkins and Tracey Regan
Artwork by Jill Barber Richardson

 A catalogue record for this
work is available from the
National Library of Australia

National Library of Australia Catalogue-in-Publication data:

Negotiate Your Worth/Sam Trattles

ISBN: 978-0-6452226-0-9 (Paperback)

ISBN: 978-0-6454076-3-1 (eBook)

Disclaimer
The publisher and the author make no guarantees concerning the level
of success you may experience by following the advice and strategies
contained in this book, and you accept the risk that results will differ for
each individual.

What people are saying about this book.....

"Tapping into the behavioural characteristics of animals has been an effective way to teach life lessons since story-telling begun. From Indigenous creation stories to Aesop's Fables, the valuable and cautionary tales that can be found in nature resonate. In 'Negotiate Your Worth', Sam has brilliantly captured the essence of some of Australia's unique and iconic wildlife. The traits that have allowed these species to be perfectly adapted to their environment can also be techniques we can employ in strategic discussion and negotiation. Sam explores this in a fun and accurate way, and has taken the time to research each of the species so that the nexus is genuine. Within 'Negotiate Your Worth' we come away with a better understanding of ourselves and the inextricable links between humans and the world around us. These links and the shared future between humans and wildlife must be protected. I thank Sam for supporting the work of Taronga through this book."
Nick Boyle, Divisional Director - Welfare, Conservation and Science, Taronga Conservation Society Australia

"Negotiate Your Worth" by Sam Trattles is knowledgeable, helpful and fun. More than words, it is skills oriented and plus you build your own unique customised negotiating tool kit. And with Sam's extensive background it is all based on proven performance results. No matter what your negotiating skill level is, this has something to offer everyone."
Susan E. Horwitz, Director, Sport NSW; Member, Faculty of the Arts, Design & Architecture Advisory Council, University of NSW; Former Director/Co-Owner, Horwitz Publications Pty Ltd

"Negotiate Your Worth is a treasure trove of practical advice, expert wisdom and useful self- evaluation activities to help business owners conquer the intimidating task of negotiating the price of their services. The workbook style and ability to amalgamate activities at the end of the book allows the reader to review and really reflect on their progress in building this vital skillset."
Jade Collins, Director, Femeconomy

What people have said about Sam's other book, *I Love Negotiating*...

"If you're like most women, negotiation is not on your list of 'love to' – but it should be on your list of 'must do.' Over the course of their lives, women leave tens of thousands of dollars on the table by not negotiating. This book not only provides solid tools and tips, it also helps you to identify the emotions that may be getting in your way of negotiating with courage and confidence. I learned something from it and I'm sure you will too!"
Lois P. Frankel, Ph.D. author of Nice Girls Don't Get the Corner Office and Nice Girls Don't Speak Up or Stand Out

To all those who have offered me: a hand, some advice, a tissue, a shoulder to lean on, a leg up, a reality check, some perspective, a kick in the pants, a glass of wine, a laugh, something other than Baked Beans, and any kind of encouragement during this new career.

Thank you!

CONTENTS

WHAT'S MY STORY, AND WHY DID I WRITE THIS BOOK

At this point, you may be thinking, 'Well this sounds exciting, and yes, I would love to learn the tools that will make me a powerful negotiator but... Who is Sam Trattles? How did she become an expert in negotiating? What skills can I learn from her? And, how can she relate to me and my small business?'.

Well, here's a little of my story. I worked for almost 20 years in corporate roles with industry giants like PricewaterhouseCoopers, Telstra, and Credit Suisse, and since leaving that behind I have been running my own service-based business.

I've negotiated over $550 million in deals to date with businesses, sports, arts, and community organisations, including SportAUS, Opera Australia, Mushroom Music, The Australian Ballet, National Rugby League, Tropfest, Australian Football League, Great Barrier Reef Foundation, Fire and Rescue NSW, Hong Kong Sevens, Olympics, Paralympics, and many more incredible brands and their leaders.

These deals taught me many things about negotiating. I've seen the good, the bad, and the ugly at the deals table over the years. One of the things that surprises many people is that you don't have to be a jerk to be a great negotiator. Being a good communicator, having a growth mindset, and viewing things from both sides of the table means you'll get great results and respect from your peers.

The day I stepped away from the corporate deals table to start out as a small business owner I had no idea of the adventure I was getting into!

The early days were exciting and challenging, a rollercoaster ride of learning and transformation. However, I had a problem. A BIG problem. I couldn't work out why I was struggling to close deals. I came from a big gig where I was doing deals every day – multi-million-dollar deals. I was at the top of my game. So, I imagined closing deals would be the least of my problems.

I found clients through my networks, friends, and referrals, so the pipeline wasn't an issue. But once I went to close the deal I'd suddenly hit a brick wall. As soon as someone questioned my rates I struggled. I didn't know what to say. And, like most people, I took it personally, got frustrated, and questioned my capabilities.

It was a shock. I couldn't believe I was doing such a bad job at securing clients. It got to the point where I was worried that I'd have to close the virtual doors of my business. I needed to take a step back, reset, and ask the question, 'What do I need to know, think, and do to be able to negotiate my worth?'.

When I stripped it back there was a significant difference in the way I had to do my new job compared to my old ones. Essentially, in my corporate roles I was given a problem to solve and told to deliver a result. Pretty straight forward. But business ownership meant I had to:

- work out what problems I could solve for other people;
- go find someone who might have these problems;
- meet with them to understand their business challenge, and
- articulate how I could help solve their problem;
- determine how long it might take to get the job done;
- price the project;
- negotiate and close the deal;
- and THEN, start delivering it!!!

This is not a pursuit for the faint-hearted, but the joy you can experience building a business around what you love to do every day makes it all worth it. Especially when it all starts to fall into place. Once I understood that my job had fundamentally changed, I could identify the 'tricky bits' of the deal, and all the parts that contributed to that, and set about ensuring I had a toolkit of assets that would support my success.

Today I feel empowered to negotiate great outcomes for my business, which means I enjoy the process; talking about money with potential clients isn't uncomfortable; and I know where I can be flexible and how to close deals efficiently. All things I know you can do too.

In 2016 I completed my first book *I Love Negotiating* – an easy-to-use workbook that guides you through the pitfalls of the process for everyday negotiations. I truly love negotiating, and the thought that it causes so many people pain doesn't sit well with me. I wish I could add it to the curriculum in every school and encourage every family and friend group to find their voice and ability to engage in more healthy debate and negotiations.

Building on my positive experiences with that book and with business leaders who regularly seek out my expertise to negotiate critical deals, I embarked on writing this book. Putting together the building blocks that have helped me overcome negotiation challenges and start achieving consistently positive results. I wanted to empower those who struggle with this most crucial part of small business ownership - negotiating your worth.

I hope this book builds your confidence at the deals table and empowers you to negotiate great commercial outcomes for your business.

I'm Sam Trattles. I help create powerful negotiators. And by working your way through this book, I know you will become one too!

So, let's get cracking.

INTRODUCTION

Negotiating your worth can be such an intimidating part of being a successful business owner but it's one of the things you need to be proficient at. Your livelihood depends on your capability to do this.

In contrast, when you have a job working for someone else, it's only about once a year that you have the uncomfortable conversation about your salary.

However, when your business is based on your intelligence, when *you are the product*, you have to negotiate your worth pretty much every day. There are few other pursuits where you have to talk about money so often with people you're not intimately involved with.

Naturally you'd be happy if someone could close deals for you so you could just get on with delivering great results. But you know it doesn't work like that, sadly there is no silver bullet.

'How do I actually know what I'm worth?' Chances are, you didn't set out to be a 'wheeler' or a 'dealer', you never saw yourself as an Entrepreneur. If you've started your own service-based business, it's likely you're damn good at what you do, and you've seen a gap in the market – so you've gone for it.

As a result, the job of consistently having to talk about money, articulating your worth, and demonstrating the value you can deliver to a potential client has been uncomfortable for you from day one.

A key part of your role as a business owner is to make money or save money, but if you hate negotiating, your effectiveness at the deals table is significantly hampered.

The process is plagued with ambiguity, with the question 'How do I actually know what I'm worth?' ringing loudly in your ears.

For you, a familiar conversation that makes you ask this question regularly, would go a little bit like this...

...you meet with a potential client, listen to their pain points, and you've worked out you can help them.

Then you make a suggestion that goes a little something like this...

...'Based on what you've told me I think the best solution I can offer is our xx program. This program takes about yy weeks to implement, and it costs $zz.'

Then, your potential client says 'THAT sentence' all business owners dread...

'Oh, that's more than I thought it might cost. '

An awkward silence fills the space as you find yourself on the back foot. There are a thousand thoughts going through your head, like:

...'Oh no, not this again.'

...'I knew I priced this too high.'

...'What do I say to change their mind?'

...'I really need this work.'

'I just wish I knew what I should say next'

...'Maybe they'll make a counter-offer, and I'll just say yes to whatever offer they make.'

...'I thought I was making a reasonable offer. Am I wrong to be charging this amount?'

...'I know this is a good deal, how do I get them to see that?'

...'Why does this example include a bit where I mention price in the first meeting, I never do that.'

...'I think they're just trying to screw me down on price, this is a tactic.'

BUT the loudest and most repeated sentence I hear from clients is ...

'I just wish I knew what I should say next (to close this deal at the rate I'm worth!)'

If you experience this often the process likely causes you to doubt your value – despite <u>all</u> the experience and knowledge you <u>know</u> you have to offer clients. Logic and rationale go out the window and you suddenly go into a mental tailspin. You freeze, become lost for words, or talk, talk, talk your way through these situations trying to justify the value you can deliver. You sit dreading 'THAT sentence' and wish you never heard a client say it ever again.….. if this is you, YOU'RE IN THE RIGHT PLACE.

If you aren't yet certain this book is for you, here are some other signs you're not feeling empowered to negotiate your worth:

- You negotiate over email, instead of having meetings face-to-face or via video conference.

- You get frustrated, react passive aggressively or with unhealthy language (even if that's just inside your head).

- Your rates are based on the mentality that, 'I reckon that's what people will pay,' instead of coming up with them based on a rigorous process.

- You don't know what to say, when to say it, and how to walk away from a poor deal, without beating yourself up.

Once you've finished reading this book you should never dread this conversation again! Because so much is riding on knowing what to say next; how you react; and when to push back.

In this book we'll unpack how you never have to dread 'THAT sentence', *"Oh, that's more than I thought it might cost."* Instead, you'll actually be anticipating it, and you'll *know* what to say next.

Negotiating your worth hinges on you knowing your worth, and throughout this practical guide you'll find ways to unlock your ability to become a powerful negotiator of your worth.

You'll know what to say next

WHAT ANIMALS HAVE TO DO WITH NEGOTIATING YOUR WORTH

Spending a lot of time at deals tables, and even more with teams and leaders preparing for them, gives me lots of opportunity to identify the skills, traits, and behaviours that contribute to being a good negotiator.

As this book is targeted to business owners, specifically to service-based business owners (consultants, agencies, etc.), it was important for me to sift through and identify what would have the greatest impact for our kinds of negotiations.

For you, I've identified the top 8 characteristics that make a *powerful negotiator*. When you get all of these characteristics to click into place, negotiating your worth will come naturally to you.

In this book I've broken down each of these characteristics so you can easily identify them, relate to them, and track how you are performing against them – which will help you know where to focus your energy to improve on them.

With each characteristic I've suggested a number of ways you can strengthen your ability to master each of them. These may be by shifting your mindset, undertaking a review, or patting yourself on the back for what you already do well when it comes to negotiating.

Pat yourself on the back

So, what's with the animals? Well, the truth is learning a new skill like negotiating can be a bit dry, so I wanted to make this learning experience fun! Once I'd identified the key negotiator powers, I sought out a parallel in nature, and found it amongst *Australian native animals*. They are often seen as cute and cuddly (which they are), however, if you take a deeper look at the skills that help them survive in the challenging Aussie environment, they are remarkably powerful.

You'll see how each of these animals are unique (just like you), and they each have wonderful skills that align with specific aspects to being a powerful negotiator (just like you can), and how these skills help them survive in what can be a tough environment (just like you do).

To help you move towards being a consistently powerful negotiator, you're going to learn the skills and capabilities that you already share with our *furry* friends, as well as those you need to work on.

WHY YOU HAVE A BLOCK WHEN IT COMES TO NEGOTIATING

Frankly, it's probably because you've never been taught how to do it well. If that's you, then cut yourself some slack. The majority of people have not learnt this skill despite it consistently being in the list of soft skills business owners and leaders' must-have, and it's noted as one of the essential skills in the World Economic Forum Future of Jobs Report.

By reading this book you're giving yourself one of the most practical lessons that your teachers could have shared, instead of the one about Pythagoras's theorem!?!

As a result of this gap in knowledge you've probably wanted to avoid negotiating as much as possible, or to kick the proverbial can down the road until you can't avoid it any longer, because it causes you anxiety. It turns out it causes a LOT of people anxiety – about 87% of people are apprehensive about negotiating, according to a recent survey from Salary.com.

Adding to this, a study by Brooks and Schweitzer from Pennsylvania University determined that anxious negotiators: set lower expectations; make lower first-offers; respond more quickly to offers; and attain worse outcomes. And I would say that's because they just want it over with.

However, while proficient negotiators still experience certain levels of anxiety, their ability to reframe the experience as an exciting challenge helps them secure better outcomes (what researchers call 'high negotiation self-efficacy'). It may not surprise you that the best strategy to improve 'self-efficacy' is through additional negotiation training. So, congratulations, once again you are facing this head on by working your way through this book.

One more block you may have, when it comes to your desire to embrace negotiating, is due to growing up in a society filled with cultural taboos. Some of these significantly impact your success as a service-based business owner, including, the fact that you're constantly having to:

- talk about money, despite it being considered rude to do so;

- articulate your worth to people you don't know by telling them all about your past successes, because this might be considered bragging;

- tell people what you want, because you could be seen as being pushy, or

- be clear about what you don't want, as it sounds like you're being difficult.

And somehow, you're supposed to secure the best deal from every negotiation!?! All these taboos make negotiating your worth exhausting – so, damn the taboos!

Damn the taboos!

If you want to become a powerful negotiator and successfully deliver great results for your business by making (more) money or saving money at the deals table, you need to find a way to push through taboos and *get comfortable having uncomfortable conversations*.

If you don't do it, you don't eat. And if you do it poorly, you end up working for less than those flipping burgers.

By sitting in the shadows and avoiding uncomfortable conversations you're making your job harder AND you're perpetuating these cultural taboos. You're missing out on revenue and you're hurting your own confidence by ignoring the problem.

The only way forward is to make a conscious decision that you <u>will</u> go after what you deserve. That you <u>will</u> push past the awkwardness. If you do, it won't be long before you find yourself feeling more comfortable, confident, and empowered to secure great results for your business.

I must warn you, the words in the pages ahead will encourage you to have many uncomfortable conversations, to push taboos aside, and to be more direct. On the upside, those conversations could be a game-changer for you and your business. You will learn to become more comfortable with open discussions about your worth. If you're feeling a little anxious, don't worry, that will fade as your confidence grows.

NEGOTIATION FUNDAMENTALS FOR A HEALTHY MINDSET

First, let's start with a small shift in language.

If you currently hate negotiating, let's start by *stopping*. **Stop referring to them as negotiations**. Change your language to simply refer to them as *conversations*, or a series of conversations. This small twist in language will help calm your mind from the outset.

Next, let's be clear, negotiating isn't a fight. It's about coming together to discuss what each of your needs and wants are. You're both trying to reach an agreement that works. Healthy debate is one thing but arguing isn't negotiating.

If you find yourself in a room where people are yelling or not listening to one another, you should end the meeting and come back together on another day when people agree to negotiate.

Negotiating isn't a fight.

Finally, and most importantly, if you're going to become a powerful negotiator, I want to challenge a long sought-after goal for your negotiations. You've probably heard of the concept that you should be 'Seeking a win:win outcome.' THIS IS A PROBLEM!

'Seeking a win:win' is a problem for your brain, this idea is fraught with danger. The word *win* triggers your primal response – your brain's fight, flight, or freeze response kicks in – signalling that you may need to prepare for the opposite.

Your physicality changes when talking about winning. You're more likely leaning in or standing on your tippy toes, getting ready to make a swift exit because your mind is thinking, 'I'm going into battle.' As a result, you *start* the process of negotiating with a heightened level of tension. Your body is looking for reasons to stay and fight, or turn and run, which is not a great start for something you cannot avoid in your job.

So if win:win is not the goal, let's get clear on the result you should be aiming for instead. I believe a good negotiation finishes with a fair and reasonable exchange of value.

A good negotiation finishes with a fair and reasonable exchange of value.

This approach invites you to start a dialogue. By asking the questions 'Is what I'm asking for fair?' and, 'Is what I want in exchange, reasonable?' and vice versa from the person we're negotiating with. This approach to the conversation will help you determine if it's a good deal for you, or if you should walk away.

The other challenge with pursuing a win:win is that it doesn't guide you through a process, it's just a concept.

So, to further support this goal I think we should be aiming to achieve, in my first book *I Love Negotiating,* I created the **APEC Framework** – an acronym that stands for: Accept, Prepare, Engage, Close. This is a simple, yet effective, 4 Stage Process for managing any negotiation, no matter how small or significant.

Every time you step into the room to negotiate a deal with a client, whether that be in a boardroom, coffee shop, over video conference or on the phone, working through my APEC Framework and the supporting PREPARE Cheat-Sheet Template will give you confidence and leave you feeling less tense. Refer to **YOUR Business Negotiator Toolkit** for more on **The Fundamentals** (more on this shortly).

These fundamentals should put you in a healthy mindset towards negotiating. Having clarity on the aim, and knowing there is a methodology to guide you, will hold you in good stead as you work your way through this book. But the key to your success is to implement change, just like learning a new language or a musical instrument, you have to practice. Neuroscientists say the best way to make new neural pathways (patterns) is through repetition and practice. That way, those connections will be established enough to become habitual or default behaviours.

HOW TO MAKE THE MOST OF THIS BOOK

How you work your way through this book is totally up to you! You can dip in and out, read it in one sitting, finish a chapter a day, or even just one page at a time – whatever works for you.

If you view this book's content as essentially a "make-good" lesson from the one you didn't get when you were at school, then consider this your negotiator textbook. (Push aside the one with Pythagoras' Theorem in it.)

It's been written to serve you over time. Keep it on a shelf at your desk so you are regularly thinking about negotiating. It will remind you that negotiating well supports your *primary function as a business owner*.

I designed it as a practical tool, something I wish someone had given me when I first started my business – because life would have been a whole lot easier if they had! As this is your textbook, one just for you, I encourage you to make notes on these pages – go on, do it – note down your thoughts, actions and learnings, so you can implement change. Then revisit your notes later to see how much your thinking and confidence has shifted.

Ok, if the thought of writing in a book doesn't work for you, visit **www. negotitateyourworth.com.au/resources,** download the tools and templates, then you can make all your notes on those pages.

To enhance the effectiveness of your learning experience, there are two key supporting elements to this book:

1. YOUR BUSINESS NEGOTIATION TOOLKIT

One of the most frustrating things about negotiating is that our brains have a habit of holding on to our 'misses' more than taking note and recognising our 'hits'!

You probably can't quickly identify the parts of the negotiating process that you're really good at, or a time you nailed a deal with confidence, but you probably could recall a time when you made a mess of one. This is normal.

In fact, researchers say negative experiences trigger increased activity in the memory sections of our brain. Many think this has evolutionary roots – for our survival we needed to notice the lion in the brush, more than we needed to notice the beautiful flower growing along the path we tread daily.

So, we need to stop relying on our brains alone to capture our positive negotiation memories. As you work your way through this book you're going to discover many things that you'll want to 'bank' for use later. To facilitate this, I've created **YOUR Business Negotiation Toolkit**.

As you'll see demonstrated so well by our *furry* friends, animals have a need to gather information about the things going on around them. A bank of knowledge which helps them eat, be more energy efficient, and stay alive. This is something they've built over time and created by observing and learning how the landscape, people, and other creatures around them react.

Knowledge is power, so having this information as a handy reference tool can add a sense of predictability and calm, making life less stressful, and negotiations less intense – so you can start to enjoy them.

YOUR Business Negotiation Toolkit – is all about you and your experiences. It has many components to it, all of which you'll get to know well as you work your way through this book. The key elements include:

YOUR ACTION PLAN
To put what you learn into action.

YOUR NEGOTIATOR LANGUAGE BANK
To ensure you have a reference bank of negotiator language that works for you.

YOUR NEGOTIATOR POWER TOOLS
To arm you with what you need to embrace the powers of each Power Animal at the deals table.

MY NEGOTIATION FUNDAMENTALS
To guide you in pursuing healthy negotiation outcomes.

When an opportunity comes up throughout this book, for you to build on **YOUR Business Negotiation Toolkit**, you'll see this icon. This means you should turn to page [123] to populate YOUR toolkit so it's personalised to your needs.

Having a personalised Toolkit will mean you're armed with what you need to overcome *your* biggest pain points in negotiating. Because you'll have:

- Evidence when things have gone well for you.
- Words, phrases, and sentences that you know you feel comfortable saying out loud.
- Clarity on situations you dread, and ways you can handle confidently.
- Tools to empower you in any situation to negotiate great outcomes for your business.

Over time you'll know exactly what to say in any negotiation situation, because you'll have this toolkit full of positive experiences you can draw on, rather than see negotiating as an activity to avoid. You'll have evidence that you're good at negotiating. Hopefully, you'll even start to enjoy yourself at the deals table.

You'll negotiate without the stress, anxiety, and pressure that is currently holding you back from being empowered to negotiate your worth. You'll no longer hear yourself saying, 'I just wish I knew what to say next to close the deal without under-selling my worth.' You'll be able to stand in your power and clearly communicate your worth, with more and more confidence every day.

2. YOUR NEGOTIATOR STRENGTHS SELF-ASSESSMENT

I know you're a busy person so, to fast track your experience, let's identify which of the characteristics of powerful negotiators you're already doing a good job at. To do that, I invite you to complete YOUR Negotiator Strengths Self-Assessment Tool in the next section.

Answering these questions will help identify your current strengths, and areas for growth, i.e. which of our incredible Australian native animal traits you embody, or which ones you need to invest more time getting to know.

With the results this book will transform into a 'choose your own adventure' book, as the results will give you a suggested pathway through the chapters.

I do recommend that you learn about each animal, but if you are in a hurry, start with those you rate yourself lowest on.

A little tip, visiting the animals that you highlight as a strength will give you an opportunity to pat yourself on the back and acknowledge your existing brilliance, which should put a pep in your negotiator step.

IDENTIFYING YOUR HIDDEN NEGOTIATOR POWERS

It's no secret that native Australian flora and fauna is unique; particularly the creatures which, at first glance, some people just see as cute and cuddly (which they can be). However the more you get to know them, the more you realise how incredibly powerful they are. Each animal has hidden powers that make them unforgettable when you realise what they're capable of when their powers are unleashed.

Much like business owners who embrace their inner negotiator powers, being underestimated at first glance can be a gift.

Once people have a second and third glance at Australia's fauna, they never underestimate them again. There is a great deal of respect for these creatures that can win your heart one minute then, if you cross them, will set you straight and ensure you never forget their powers.

Having coached and trained hundreds of business leaders, I feel most are being 'cute and cuddly' in their approach to negotiating. Perhaps you're in this state now.

So, it's time we expose your inner powers. You can become a consistently good negotiator, and when you do, you will be a force to be reckoned with, just as these animals are.

EIGHT CHARACTERISTICS OF POWERFUL NEGOTIATORS

Let's look at the iconic Australian creatures I've selected to help unleash your inner powerful negotiator. We'll learn more about the characteristics they possess and the lessons they have to share with us.

For each we'll explore what they are known for at first glance, then take a deeper look at their real powers and identify how these traits provide a lesson for you as a business owner.

FRILL-NECKED LIZARD
Finding BRAVERY within

KOOKABURRA
PATIENTLY unlocking the JOY

WOMBAT
Being clear on BOUNDARIES

BRUSHTAIL POSSUM
Identifying predictable PATTERNS

EIGHT CHARACTERISTICS OF POWERFUL NEGOTIATORS

RED KANGAROO
TRAILBLAZING your path

BILBY
Harnessing your RESILIENCE

EMU
Being boldy CURIOUS

PLATYPUS
Being sensitive to enable FLEXIBILITY

The awesome Aussie animals that possess these characteristics:

Kookaburra

PATIENTLY unlocking the JOY

'*Laugh Kookaburra, Laugh Kookaburra*', '*Merry, merry king of the bush is he*'...what a wonderful thing to be known as. Their uplifting laugh makes Kookaburras appear to be able to find the **joy** in everything. It seems they look at the world and see the funny side to it.

Alas we may be **underestimating** our friend the Kookaburra. While their ability to make us laugh is a superpower in itself, another hidden power is their 'sit and wait' technique of hunting. They wait **patiently** for prey to pass by and then swoop down from their high perches to grab food and crush it in their strong beaks. They also have excellent vision which works hand-in-hand with the sit and wait technique.

...For you this means more success will come your way by being patient and purposefully enjoying the experience along the way. This will help you be more aware of what you can expect to happen and know when to swoop when an **opportunity** presents itself. Though, let's leave the 'crushing with your beak' part strictly to the Kookaburra!

Brushtail Possum

Identifying predictable PATTERNS

Known as a fluffy, nocturnal visitor to our urban homes, the 'Common' Brushtail Possum has a prehensile tail for curling around branches like a monkey, helping them to swing from tree to tree, then noisily rattle across our rooftops every night.

Possums are harmless despite their sharp claws, and their hidden powers are in how they have become **highly adapted** to urban living. Coming into contact with people so often has led them to **adjust** their lifestyle, learning from the **repeated patterns of predictable behaviours** of their neighbours. They've adapted to take advantage of what their 'neighbours' leave for them to forage.

Our beautiful Possums offer you **encouragement** to consider your **environment** and what lessons are all around that can guide you on your path. Taking your time, looking for the signs, habits, and regularities to your own and your clients' behaviours, will make it easier when negotiating your worth.

Bilby

Harnessing your RESILIENCE

To support their plight for survival after 15 million years of existence, the Bilby has been embraced as Australia's alternative to the Easter Bunny, after being on the brink of extinction.

Although small, they roam large, arid areas, and they personify resilience. They are extremely hard-working – excavating extensive deep burrows, managing up to 12 burrows at any one time, helping them to keep their options open.

They are known as 'ecosystem engineers' because they shape the environment with their digging. Over the course of a year an individual Bilby can turn over more than 3 tonne of soil per year!

....The world of business ownership can feel like a lonely pursuit, however, our mate the Bilby is here to remind you to look around and see that **you're not alone**, there are lots of champions 'on your **team**' that you can rely on to support your decisions (and negotiations).

Additionally, it's good to regularly reflect on the Bilby's ability to **survive** tough times. Always being open to create options is required to survive in your own ever-evolving environment will help you through difficult times.

Platypus

Being sensitive to enable FLEXIBILTY

Famous for being so **unusual**, our Platypus is an extremely shy, solo dwelling monotreme. Upon discovery British scientists thought they were a hoax as they are so unique. These days they are often referred to as a cross between a Beaver and a Duck, but they are so much more.

Their greatest hidden power is that they have a **sixth sense** – Electroreception. They are **highly sensitive** to everything around them: other creatures, people, and their ever-changing environment. Being so **aware** helps the Platypus steer clear of challengers. The Platypus is, in fact, Australia's only venomous furred animal, but due to their hyper-sensitive powers they only throw their venom at times of high agitation or unpredictability.

The Platypus is a symbol that you don't have to be loud to be powerful. Instead, you can channel your efforts into being more **sensitive to your environment** – the economic landscape shifts, your clients, and those around you.

Your core strength in a negotiation is in having complete confidence in **how you came up with your rates**. If you get this right, you can be dangerous but controlled, just like our furry friend.

Emu

Being boldly
CURIOUS

The Emu is a notably tall, flightless bird who is an ambassador for our nation, standing **proud** on the Commonwealth Coat of Arms as a symbol of **progress**, because they cannot walk backwards easily.

Their powers of **curiosity** can be underestimated, as they boldly explore what they see. They are inclined to get up-close and personal to the things before them, seemingly **unafraid** to face whatever is in front of them. Imagine coming face to face with an Emu knowing they can't back off!

...The Emu offers an invitation for you to **be bold and curious**, to not shy away from opportunities, to ask questions, to talk about money, or to leave the table with ambiguity.

Red Kangaroo

TRAIL-
BLAZING
your path

Known as the iconic symbol of Australia, the big Red represents our young nation of **strong** characters, who are **entrepreneurial** in nature. They thrive in our expansive, tough yet beautiful, wide, brown land.

Big Reds represent us in so many ways. In line with their hidden powers, as the **leaders** of their mob, they are trailblazers, forging their own path. As they traverse vast areas of unchartered territory, being conservative with their energy is a must for survival.

...Similarly, as a business owner you are **forging your own path**; you're the boss, so stand in your power. By knowing what you want, what you need to do to survive, and who you want to work with, you can *walk away* from a deal when you know it isn't right for you.

Wombat

Being clear on
BOUNDARIES

Wombats are known to be slow moving, a bit cuddly, and very cute ground dwellers that eat roots and leaves.

Their greatest strength comes from being a staunch defender of their home. They set **strong boundaries** that they clearly **let others know about**. The perimeter of a Common or Bare-nosed Wombat's territory is marked with square shaped droppings, so you're in no doubt you're entering their 'zone.'

During bushfires Wombats are known to let other animals shelter in their burrows. This demonstrates they are open to letting others in, however, it's **on their terms.**

For you, knowing your own boundaries and your no-go areas means that you can be **firm in negotiations**, and say no when a deal isn't right for you.

Being clear on what terms you will accept in a deal, and those you won't, gives you **strength and security**.

Frill-necked Lizard

Finding
BRAVERY
within

Considered as a bit of an enigma, Frill-necked Lizards are well known for their crazy running style, officially known as bipedal locomotion. Though small in stature, they do a great job of **appearing larger** when startled; at this point, they rise on their hind legs, unfurl a colourful frill, and ensure their predators don't underestimate them.

One of their most significant hidden talents is that they invest time in 'basking in the sun', to maintain optimum temperature, every day.

...For you, the Frill-necked Lizard is a reminder to take a step back to **reflect** on what's going on within yourself and what's going on around you, every day. By embodying 'Lizzie's' behaviours, your bravery will shine, your **self-belief will grow**, and you'll be able to step up to play a bigger game when **opportunities** present themselves.

Throughout this book I'm going to help you unlock your inner negotiator powers. To bring this to life I invite you to complete **YOUR Negotiator Strengths Self-Assessment** in the next section to help identify which animal's behaviours you are currently embracing the most, and the least.

YOUR NEGOTIATOR STRENGTHS SELF-ASSESSMENT

It's time to identify where your negotiator strengths lie, and to discover where you should focus your energy to improve your business negotiation capabilities. This approach will provide you with the shortest path through this book.

The questions on the following pages have been designed to help you identify specific patterns and behaviours you demonstrate that are impacting your success at the deals table.

You may find some that you're nailing, others you've started to address through challenges you face, then there are those that you know you're not good at and may be avoiding.

This self-assessment process is about the negotiator you are today, not the one you want to be, so as you work your way through each statement, sit in it, take your time to reflect on your typical response and give it a true assessment rating. It may be challenging, but be honest.

Once you've completed your self-assessment there are more instructions on how the results will turn this book into a 'choose your own adventure' style reading experience. Meaning you may not even have to read this whole book – yay!... time back in your day... one of the things we all appreciate.

Assessment Scale

Over the coming pages there are a series of questions. Read through each one then think about how much the behaviour or situation sounds like you.

Consider if this sounds: least like you; a bit like you; or like you most of the time – in most situations around and at the deals table.

Take your time, but don't over think it.

In the box next to the question write down how you score it on this scale:

Take a guess

For a bit of fun, before you start, think about which Power Animal you relate to most according to the hidden powers you share.

Based on the animal summaries, where do you feel your negotiator powers currently lie?

I think I share the powers of:

_____

POWER ANIMAL	QUESTION	SCORE
Kookaburra *Patience*	I enjoy my time at the deals table, I find the process of negotiating fun.	
	I'm clear on how long it usually takes to close a deal so I'm patient throughout the process.	
	I observe more than I speak at the deals table, so I know when to swoop on opportunities to close.	
	When a potential client says, 'that's more than I thought it would cost?' I have a go-to response.	
	I feel anxious-excited about closing deals, but I have a process so I don't rush it.	

TOTAL: _____

POWER ANIMAL	QUESTION	SCORE
Brushtail Possum *Patterns*	I invest time to review each deal so I learn from them – noting what I've done well and what I can build on for next time.	
	I'm conscious of typical comments/ phrases clients say in a negotiation that are an indicator I should or shouldn't pursue the deal.	
	My business has a clearly defined Ideal Client Profile – I know the types of clients I like to work with.	
	I look for patterns in the behaviours of our clients, so I am more comfortable when preparing to negotiate with them.	
	When I lose a deal, I know it's not personal, even though it's my intelligence I'm selling – it's just business.	

TOTAL: _____

THIS SOUNDS LIKE ME:

1 = LEAST   **2 = A BIT**   **3 = MOSTLY**

POWER ANIMAL	QUESTION	SCORE
Bilby *Resilience*	I have a network of supporters who help me do my best work in this lonely pursuit of business ownership.	
	I take a flexible approach to creating client solutions to meet their budget, without compromising my revenue.	
	My products have been built to be tailored, not created from scratch each time, so I can negotiate a rate on the spot.	
	I'm clear on different ways to package the products I offer clients to get a deal over the line.	
	I know how long my products take to deliver and negotiate rates accordingly.	

TOTAL: _____

POWER ANIMAL	QUESTION	SCORE
Platypus *Flexibility*	I feel confident to negotiate my worth because my fees were created based on solid research.	
	I never fear the deals table because I have everything I need to step up with confidence.	
	I embrace uncomfortable conversations, like talking about money, because they are a vital part of business success —taboos be damned!	
	I have a documented rate card with tolerances (revenue margins) so I can negotiate easily.	
	I'm sensitive to trends in my industry and the economy and can adapt swiftly (as required).	

TOTAL: _____

THIS SOUNDS LIKE ME:

1 = LEAST   **2 = A BIT**   **3 = MOSTLY**

POWER ANIMAL	QUESTION	SCORE
Emu *Curiosity*	I never leave meetings with questions left un-answered, because I'm curious and I don't mind 'looking silly' because I ask lots of them.	
	I make a point of raising the topic of fees in the first meeting with a potential client.	
	I don't have to wing it or think on my feet, because I have a process to prepare for each negotiation.	
	I aim to close 'in the room' rather than invest time writing up a proposal and sending it via email for clients to consider.	
	When clients say, 'that's more than I wanted to spend' I usually suggest 'taking things out of the bucket,' rather than discounting my fees to fit their budget.	

TOTAL: _____

POWER ANIMAL	QUESTION	SCORE
Red Kangaroo *Trail-Blazing*	I'm happy to make the tough decisions as the leader of the business, not feeling like the business is happening to me.	
	I happily turn down a project that doesn't sit well 'in my gut.'	
	I often ponder the cost of spending time with my kids/dog/friends versus working for less than I'm worth.	
	I will walk away when a client is pushing too hard on the price.	
	I tend to refer work to others when I work out a client doesn't need my core services, instead of thinking 'I'll just Google how to do it.'	

TOTAL: _____

THIS SOUNDS LIKE ME:

1 = LEAST   **2 = A BIT**   **3 = MOSTLY**

POWER ANIMAL	QUESTION	SCORE
Wombat *Boundaries*	I'm clear on my boundaries when it comes to fee tolerances.	
	I have a number of ways to say no to potential clients when a deal isn't right for my business.	
	I regularly feel my 'people pleaser gene' holds me back from saying what I really mean to clients.	
	I feel comfortable saying no to things that I really don't want to do.	
	If I have agreed to a deal that turns out not to work for my business, I'm comfortable to set a meeting to address this.	

TOTAL: _____

POWER ANIMAL	QUESTION	SCORE
Frill-necked Lizard *Bravery*	I feel confident articulating my worth at the deals table, no matter who I'm negotiating with.	
	I allocate time to review my approach to negotiating good deals regularly.	
	I will often go after really big projects as a test of my abilities.	
	I take risks with a view to grow and flex, so I continue to enjoy being a business owner.	
	I make a point of celebrating when I have done an outstanding job on behalf of my business.	

TOTAL: _____

OVERALL SCORE: _____

THIS SOUNDS LIKE ME:

1 = LEAST   **2 = A BIT**   **3 = MOSTLY**

INTERPRETING THE RESULTS OF YOUR STRENGTHS SELF-ASSESSMENT

The animal you scored highest identifies your current area of strength when it comes to negotiating your worth. Knowing you have these powers should help you feel more confident and continue to build on the characteristics you naturally demonstrate when negotiating.

Meanwhile, the animal you scored lowest identifies the area you appear to have the most difficulty with, or often avoid, when negotiating your worth. The chapter aligned with this animal will help strengthen your capability in this area, so you'll be able to embrace your new-found inner negotiator powers.

CREATING YOUR PERSONALISED TABLE OF CONTENTS

As this book is YOUR learning adventure, you can read it in any order you wish. However, there are two animals that have powers that we all should invest time to embody – the KOOKABURRA and the FRILL NECKED-LIZARD. For that reason, no matter what you scored for these animals, I suggest that you read these chapter first and last respectively.

I then recommend you **read the chapters in the order that you scored them,** from the power animal you scored lowest through to the one you scored highest. That way you'll start with the areas of greatest need and get to the areas you've already got strength in over time.

For example, if your total score for the Bilby was the lowest then I suggest you read this chapter first. And if your powers aligned highly with the big Red Kangaroo then you can read this chapter towards the end.

To make this easy for you, use the table on the next page to create your personalised table of contents.

My Personalised Table of Contents

The order I will read this book is:

YOUR chapter order	Power Animal	Hidden Power
MY chapter 1	**Kookaburra**	PATIENTLY unlocking the JOY
MY chapter 2 (lowest score)		
MY chapter 3		
MY chapter 4		
MY chapter 5		
MY chapter 6		
MY chapter 7 (highest score)		
MY chapter 8	**Frill necked-Lizard**	Finding BRAVERY within

Overall score

It may also help you to know how to interpret your overall score. This may be particularly helpful for you to refer back to and see how far you have progressed with your overall negotiator powers, over time. If your overall score is...

100 - 120	You're doing a good job and are confident to negotiate your worth. This book is likely going to be an opportunity to fine tune your approach to negotiating deals.
50 - 100	It's likely you have some strengths and a few areas that require some support with when it comes to negotiating your worth. You'll find working your way through this book and taking action will have a big impact on your success and confidence.
40 - 50	You really need to focus on building your negotiation capabilities. As a business owner, securing revenues and positive outcomes from deals is your job and it's probably costing you a great deal (in revenues, and anxiety) – read on.

Now it's time for you to get stuck in, use your personalised table of contents to guide your way through the next section of this book.

Enjoy your adventure!

KOOKABURRA

· ·

PATIENTLY unlocking the JOY

The key characteristic that makes a Kookaburra so powerful is in viewing the world from a different, more light-hearted, perspective. They are calm, patient, and seem to enjoy seeing the madness around them. They get noticed for their big, loud laugh, which draws attention their way. However, they spend the bulk of their time engaged in a silent, 'sit and wait' technique of hunting and observing what is going on around them - then they strike!

For you to harness your inner Kookaburra powers, in the pursuit of becoming a consistently good negotiator, you could start by viewing negotiating as a game. Like all games, it should be fun. There may be times when it can be uncomfortable, but you're looking for the parts of the game that feel effortless for you – that's when it becomes really fun.

Like all gameplay, being calm and patient pays off. But when thinking about negotiating, calm isn't necessarily the first word that comes to mind for most people. However, you can shift this by understanding the patience that is required in negotiations.

A typical negotiation takes time. They are rarely a short, sharp transaction, unless you have commoditised your products. Deal-making can happen in a few meetings, or it can take months and require meeting after meeting after meeting. So, developing your 'patience muscle', like the Kookaburra, is a key factor in supporting your success.

Patience goes hand in hand with the skills of observation. Like you should, Kookaburras invest time in knowing the creatures and their behaviours that surround them, and any subtle changes that provide opportunities.

The behaviours of those you're negotiating with provide you clues with what's important to them, and where there are opportunities for you to capitalise on. These may be detected through:

BODY LANGUAGE

You want to be looking out for what their body is telling you - if they're leaning into the conversation or sitting back with folded arms. Determine if they could be cold or if this is an indicator that they aren't 'into' the conversation. Take your time to observe everyone in the room, to regularly gauge the tone of what's going on for the collective throughout the interaction. Determine if this is going well or if you need to change tact.

WHAT THEY KEEP SAYING

When you're in the room you want to be doing a lot of listening. The other party can give you strong clues about what matters to them that you can pick up on by listening out for a particular turn of phrase. If they are repeating key points in different ways, this is a point that matters to them. This will help you decide if it seems you are going to be able to reach agreement with them or if you can't satisfy their requirements.

WHAT THEY'RE NOT SAYING

How they explain things that you feel are important, such as timelines, deliverables, or money. If they are rushing through it, versus talking it through patiently, is an indicator that they are uncomfortable with some of this and you can take some comfort in that. Use it as an opportunity to call out and take the lead through the sticky parts of the deal.

This observation technique is fundamental to improving your success at the deals table.

Silence is your friend.

Another contributing factor to unlock and channel your inner Kookaburra is to understand that silence is your friend and it provides you with the opportunity to really see what's going on. By being ok with not filling the air with noise, you will find the space you need to look for clues, so you can be in a strong position to 'strike' when the time is right for you.

The more you incorporate these characteristics into your process, the more comfortable you'll become in stepping up to the deals table. Along the way, things may go off track a little, but over time you'll find the fun in the roller coaster ride, instead of getting frustrated by it. You may even start to enjoy the process.

BIGGER PICTURE TO OBSERVE

There are so many challenges to our survival in business, but the events of 2020 and beyond provide an invitation to really think like a Kookaburra. We don't find too much joy when our world is turned upside down. But taking time to observe what's going on in the market and adjusting your business, your approach to products, and how you negotiate outcomes, must be done regularly (pandemic or no pandemic).

This may result in offering completely different products or services than you do today or running a business that doesn't look anything like you planned in the early days. We don't know the full impact the events of 2020+ offer us, but they provide an opportunity to step back from what we are doing, think about what matters, and consider where you can find the joy amongst the madness of business ownership.

There will always be challenges. None of us stay in business for long without that realisation. However, the ducking and diving, and the weaving and pivoting, is what we do without thinking. It's in the reflection of this madness that we find the lessons. We look back to move forward with a spring in our step, after patting ourselves on the back.

Laughter, joy, and a different perspective on all that you do can help you through the challenges ahead.

MINDSET TIP

To help embrace this mindset consider these words from Sir Richard Branson:

"Some 80% of your life is spent working. You want to have fun at home; why shouldn't you have fun at work?"

TAKING STEPS TOWARDS FINDING THE JOY

 To help you find the joy in negotiating your worth we're going to start building **YOUR Negotiator Language Bank, POWER TOOL 1**.

Sadly, I can't give you a script for every negotiation. My words won't always work for you, and unless I'm in the room negotiating with you, or on your behalf, the chances that you'll actually say them out loud is limited, (although my consultancy wouldn't mind the revenue for me being on-call for all your negotiations).

So if this is going to work, if you're going to become a powerful negotiator, you need to capture your language, and you need to identify when you've done a great job, where you're confident and comfortable.

Also, you need to consider the times when you look back and cringe (or laugh) when the world was offering you a lesson in how *not* to do something.

Identifying your strengths and areas for growth provide a base to build on so you can start to claim your power.

Using the template in the Toolkit let's capture your initial thoughts on negotiating. Note down a time you've nailed a negotiation:

- Who was it with, what happened, what did you say or do?
- Now, try and think of more and note them down too.
- Try and get specific about the part of the discussion that went the way you had thought about in your head.
- What are the parts that you enjoy or get excited about?

Next, note the parts of negotiating that make you uncomfortable:

- Which part of the process makes you feel awkward or want to avoid?
- Why is it making you uncomfortable?
- What are your 'watch outs' - things to be mindful of - things you say, or do?
- If you're not sure, really observe your behaviour over the next week and jot this down. Then, consider ways you can shift this – what would help you feel more confident?

With your initial thoughts and feelings captured you'll see patterns of your behaviour that identify the times, places, and people when you negotiate with an air of calm. With these in mind, you can build on them and bring that feeling to the table more often.

With this starting point you can continue to populate **YOUR Negotiator Language Bank** over time. You can even refer back to this when you've finished working your way through this book, to see how much progress you've made.

WRAPPING IT UP

Evolving your inner KOOKABURRA strength comes by being a little more patient and enjoying the experience along the way. Being more aware of what's going on in the room for everyone, listening, and embracing silence will help you know 'when to swoop' on an opportunity, making the whole experience more comfortable and joyful for you.

ACTION PLAN

There are a number of things you can put into place after getting to know the KOOKABURRA, and I'm sure you'll get to these over time, but to ensure the effort you put into reading these pages converts for you...

What's the ONE action you'll take to harness your inner KOOKABURRA?

BRUSHTAIL POSSUM

PATTERNS of predictable behaviours

Our Brushtail Possum mates are everywhere in built-up parts of Australia. For many they can be just a noisy night-time visitor running across our roof-tops, which they are, but they are also an incredibly insightful 'neighbour' for us to learn from. Their hidden power is in their ability to adapt to the opportunities that present themselves every day. Possums look for patterns; things they can predict, react to, and rely upon for their survival.

For you to embrace your inner Possum, we're going to dig into the patterns you have created *over time* as a business owner, helping you be more conscious about the ways you respond well to certain situations. We'll also look deeper into the behaviours of your clients, which will enable you to understand how they will typically react, unlocking ways to stand in your power at the deals table.

By doing this you will be able to make some assumptions, predict behaviours, and feel comfortable that you know what to say in a negotiation when the time is right. You won't feel like you're always reacting. Instead, your inner Possum will empower you to think, 'I've got this, I know what is likely to happen when dealing with a client or situation like this.'

Now we're going to work through ways you can unlock your inner Possum powers.

REVIEWING YOUR LAST 10 DEALS

Let's take some time to reflect over the last 10 deals that have come across your desk. As we work through the rest of this chapter, think like a Possum – you're looking to identify the behaviours, patterns, and regularities that might predict future behaviours. You want to find the things that people say to you, often. The particular words, phrases, or reactions that are repeated patterns of behaviour in the people (or types of clients) you negotiate with regularly.

BUT first things first – be crystal clear, you are going to lose deals. It's unrealistic for anyone to expect a 100% win rate. Be kind to yourself and cut yourself some slack right off the bat. It's disappointing when you're unsuccessful but understanding why makes the loss less painful.

In the early days, it's easy to think a rejection from a potential client is a rejection about how good you are at what you do. One of the most comforting realities is to know that losing is not personal, it really is *just business*. The further along your business ownership career you travel, the better you become at decoupling the outcome of a deal from your personal abilities in your field of expertise.

You may feel that a lost deal is a lost deal and moving on to the next thing is more important than pulling it apart to discover why. However, I want to help you see that with a change in mindset, you can learn a lot from what you've done in the past.

By being aware of what you've done well in the negotiation and what felt effortless, you will be able to replicate those times and tweak the others, giving you more confidence in future negotiations.

Find opportunities to celebrate your brilliance.

Whenever possible, find opportunities to celebrate your brilliance. This may give you some renewed energy, and a pep in your step, to keep going in this crazy thing called business ownership.

DEALS YOU'VE WON

When you think about a few of the recent deals you've won, hopefully the first thing you take from these is a sense of pride and achievement. Well done. When you're in the business of closing deals and rely on a positive outcome for the food on your table, every win should be celebrated.

Not wanting to be a Negative Nancy, but let's view these deals in another light to see if you can take even more from them. Take a look at each successful deal and ask yourself:

- If the call for that work came in today, would you do it all the same again? If not, what would you change?

- Now that you have rolled out the work, if you could reprice the job would you have priced it differently?

- When you place yourself in the room, is there a chance you could have gotten a little more from the exchange at the deals table?

Take note of your reflections and lay out some actions to implement in future deals. Test a few things, tweak your language a little, or change the way you ask for things, and see what happens.

DEALS YOU'VE LOST

There are no two ways about it, losing deals sucks. There's so much effort invested in trying to secure revenues, so when the outcome doesn't go your way it's disappointing.

But as a glass half-full kind of person, which most business owners are, there are valuable lessons to be taken from these situations. Step through each deal you were unsuccessful in and ask yourself:

- Looking back on the situation, are you clear on why you were unsuccessful? If not, could you ask the client a few questions to get clarity?

- Do you know the competitor you lost the deal to? Sometimes this can turn out to be a win in itself. You may want to ask who you're pitching against or who you lost the deal to, so you know if you have cause to celebrate. If you find you missed out to a bigger brand or team, celebrate it. In context, coming runner up to Superwoman *is* a win.

- Do you get the impression it was a complete waste of your time? Sometimes clients want to know they have a good deal from their current supplier by comparing a number of others. You may want to add a step to your process to help you stop wasting time. Simply ask *why* the job is going to market then you can make a more informed decision whether to pitch or not to pitch.

- Had you already won the deal in your head before they came back to confirm either way? If a potential client sought you out and asked you to pitch saying something like, 'Would you please pitch, as I'm not sure the other teams will get it,' then this may give a strong indicator that you are likely to succeed. BUT be warned, this could also be a red herring - one that we've all fallen for. It's a shock when we are unsuccessful and it hurts twice as much because we have already started spending the money in our head, or feel we have wasted time, or perhaps we didn't put enough effort in due to being over-confident. Remember, it's not over until the gorgeously voluptuous lady is singing up a storm, so never take anything as a given.

CLOSING OR ROLLING OVER ON DEALS

It's important to identify if you're actually closing deals or if you're rolling over to avoid uncomfortable conversations.

What I mean by that is, how often do you stick to the valuation you put on a project? If you say the project will cost $10,000 and the client says, 'How about $8,000?' and you concede without a second thought.

That's not closing a deal. That's rolling over.

In this common scenario it's often about avoiding having to have an uncomfortable conversation about money, by just saying yes.

Have an uncomfortable conversation about money.

If instead you enter the deal knowing the value you bring to the client and can demonstrate a willingness to be flexible because you know how much 'fat' you have to play with, then that's closing a deal.

When you successfully close deals by securing a fair price for the value you bring to the table, your confidence will rise. By avoiding the exchange, you miss that opportunity.

Always look out for these opportunities and take note of how your behaviour and confidence evolves.

IT'S NOT PERSONAL - LESSONS IN REJECTION

A rejection of the work you're proposing is not a rejection of, or reflection on, you personally.

When a potential client tells you that your fees are too high (for them), you may start to worry and think, 'I am the product here so, how can I not take this personally?'.

Taking things personally can cause us to poorly manage questions, queries, or requests from clients because we feel it's a personal attack on our worth. It's not. It's about someone taking money out of their wallet to buy your brain's capabilities. If you are clear on the value of their investment, and have determined the cost of that value, you will find ways to disconnect a negative outcome from a personal rejection.

I'm not saying this is easy - it's just a fact. Finding ways to put yourself at arm's length from the outcome of the negotiation will help.

Consider how you feel when you negotiate on behalf of someone else, perhaps your mum, sister, or an employee. It's not as stressful right? That's because you're acting on behalf of someone else, and you're asking for it because you know they deserve it.

Well, you need to capture that approach when negotiating for yourself. The reality is you *are* negotiating on behalf of someone else, well, something else – it's on behalf of your business, your bank account, your family, and your pantry. If you can take away the assumption that it's 'all about you' and don't take it personally, then you'll find some clarity.

It's disappointing when we don't secure a potential client, but the one who makes it personal is us! We kick ourselves for what we should have done or should have said. When you believe you didn't do anything wrong – it's more likely that they have conflicting budget priorities, the timing isn't right for them, or they aren't your ideal client so were never going to be able to work with you.

Instead of kicking yourself with the shoulda, woulda, coulda's, how about you ask them why your scope of work or proposal was rejected? If you don't you risk beating yourself up for weeks or months wondering. This can make you gun-shy at the deals table, risking future losses, as you may think the service, i.e. your expertise, isn't of value.

The reality is that within each market, there are different people looking for different services, at different price points, with very different expectations on the value they expect in exchange for that.

If you do miss out on a deal, instead of shying away, get back on the phone. Set up 10 coffee meetings. If you have 10 more rejections, perhaps then you can consider the viability of the product or the appetite in the market for what you're putting out there; you may need to 'retire' that product or pivot your offering.

If you don't get a high percentage of rejections, take the lessons and stay the course.

MINDSET TIP

To help embrace this mindset consider the words in Don Miguel Ruiz's insightful book, *The Four Agreements.* The Second Agreement is: Don't Take Anything Personally.

Ruiz states that, *'Nothing others do is because of you. What others say and do is a projection of their own reality, their own dream,'* and *'There is a huge amount of freedom that comes to you when you take nothing personally.'*

WHO YOU WANT TO WORK WITH

Now let's look deeper into the type of clients you are chasing. This would typically be identified in your Ideal Client Profile: a summary of the client you love to work with, crafted from what you know to be true about them and their behaviours. It would typically be created as part of your marketing plan, so check your marketing strategy.

Think about your Ideal Client Profile. Now overlay that with the same deals you were just considering. Next think like a Possum - look for what you can predict: the common repeatable outcomes, conversations or reactions that you can lean on for preparation and confidence moving forward.

BEHAVIOURS OF YOUR IDEAL CLIENT

There is a lot of pain that comes from talking to potential customers who are not aligned to your service levels, products, or pricing. These tend to be the conversations that end with the sentence, 'What you're offering is just way too expensive.'; or the ones where you walk away from the negotiation feeling like a failure.

It doesn't have to be that way. If you're having these conversations regularly it's probably them, not you. You're just not working with your ideal client. You're likely to be talking to the wrong people about what you offer. Without clarity on who you serve best you will continue to scratch your head, wondering why you're struggling to get deals over the line and why clients are pushing back on what you feel is fair and reasonable.

By identifying the type of businesses and leaders that benefit most from what you offer, at the price you feel it's worth, your success rate should naturally increase. For example, if you're pitching a premium product you should build a profile that aligns to those looking for a high-end solution. Meanwhile, if you're offering a quick and/or easy solution your ideal client will look, think, and act very differently.

To build your Ideal Client Profile, engage a marketer, or start by creating an outline of who they are. Think of your favourite client, their drivers, the challenges they typically face, the complexity of their solutions, the companies they work in, their role, etc. Build this profile with as much detail as you can, you can even give them a name.

This isn't a silver bullet, but it certainly helps your confidence when you are aligning with your ideal client. If you are losing work, at least it will be for the right reasons, and not because the client could never really afford your service or appreciate the value you deliver. Perhaps they were only ever looking for a cheap or quick solution in the first place.

WHAT YOUR IDEAL CLIENTS' SAY

 To help you identify the clients you enjoy working with, you can capture the **Behaviours of YOUR Ideal Client, *POWER TOOL 2*.**

Identify a list of 'things my clients say'.

If you are working with clients you like, you should be able to identify a list of 'things my clients say,' or perhaps 5 reactions they regularly have when you negotiate with them.

You're looking for the common words, phrases, questions, or body language 'tells' that reassure you they are your ideal client; their needs, wants, and expectations are aligned with what you deliver.

WHAT THEY DON'T SAY

Knowing the typical behaviours of your ideal client and being ready for their response is key to your success. It will also be helpful to know the clear indicators when they are NOT your ideal client.

Note down the questions you can ask to confirm whether they are, or are not, a person you want to work with. Add these words and phrases to your Power Tool, so you can recognise them when the time comes.

It will also be useful to note when you have what *you* consider, is the ideal response to each of these.

Perhaps the solutions you offer are high end and solve unique problems. You could ask a potential client something like, 'Are you looking for a bespoke solution or something more off-the-shelf?'. Depending on the response, you can say, 'Let me introduce you to Garry, he often works with people who are looking for a more off-the-shelf solution that might align better with your budget.'

This is not about negotiating. This is about choosing to work with the right people, and not the ones that aren't aligned with your expectations and budgets.

Choosing to work with the right people (for you).

Be aware that who you thought was your ideal client might not be. It's time to reconsider who your ideal client really is and drill down on the people you want to work with. For example, if you don't want to hear, 'Gosh, you're expensive' every day – don't work with micro-businesses. You know that's what they are going to say. It's not that they don't value what you do, it's just that smaller businesses are usually run on a needs-basis – 'if I spend the money on this, I can't pay for that.' And sometimes, 'that' is their wages.

If you love working with micro-businesses, you'll know this is a typical 'first response,' no matter what price you put on the table. When you know this, and want to work with these clients, you can be ready with your standard response and know how the conversation will unfold from there.

WRAPPING IT UP

By embracing your inner BRUSHTAIL POSSUM you'll view your encounters with similar types of people differently. As a result, you'll adjust your approach, based on the learning from the repeated patterns of predictable behaviours of these people.

Considering your environment and seeking the lessons all around will guide you on your path. Take your time to look for the signs, habits, and regularities to your own and your client's behaviours. This will make it easier to negotiate your worth.

ACTION PLAN

What's the ONE action you'll take to harness your inner BRUSHTAIL POSSUM?

_____

BILBY

Harnessing your RESILIENCE

The key characteristic that makes a Bilby so powerful is its resilience. While the Bilby is unlikely to know how close to extinction they have come, their ability to survive in un-imaginable parts of this country is impressive. The arid lands in the central regions don't offer much, so survival is about taking advantage of opportunities as they arise, preparing for the future, being methodical and curious.

So too is the life of a business owner.

Statistics show that surviving in business isn't easy; the Australian Bureau of Statistics states that survival rate for small businesses is about 50 percent. With the abundance of challenges, diversity of required skills and lack of resources, it is no-doubt a game for those with some ticker.

Australia has truly been a lucky country with 28 years of growth until 2020, with just a small blip during the Global Financial Crisis. However, the coming years may sadly see many businesses unable to survive.

For many industries, flexiblity proves to be a consistently key influencer in survival during significant market downturns. These times test our abilities as business owners, as we must take advantage of opportunities, adapt to the changing environment, as well as continue to prepare for our future (one that scientists say is likely to include future pandemics).

Being truly open to creating new opportunities is one of the best qualities of a smaller business, so embrace this, get help if you need it, and look around at those who are there to support you to grow through adversity.

Taking cues from the Bilby, let's identify ways to harness your resilience and take pride in what an open mindset can unlock for your business.

MINDSET TIP

To help embrace this mindset, consider Jim Rohn's quote from his book *The Five Major Pieces to the Life Puzzle:*

"Inspiration, from whatever the source, arouses feelings within us that rekindle hope, ambition, and determination. It is a momentary whisper of encouragement and reassurance that causes us to become aware of our potential."

YOU'RE NOT ALONE IN BUSINESS

While your resilience develops to changes and challenges, there is a trap for 'new players.' Like the Bilby, it is highly likely that you have a crew of supporters who can help you survive. Don't struggle on your own. If necessary, build a group of trusted advisors you can turn to.

 To help you identify the team you have to support you in business and how they help you, build out the template on the **POWER TOOL 3: Identify YOUR Support Crew.**

To identify your support crew, start by looking at the people you turn to on a tough day, and the people you pay to help you run your business. These might include: a business buddy, mentor, champion, business coach, your accountant, bookkeeper, marketing supporter, admin, best friend, your mum or dad, and the list goes on.

These people can help bring perspective, be the voice of reason, and provide a sounding board to bounce things off. They can help you make sound business decisions, pick you up when work becomes overwhelming, and support you in times that involve significant negotiations.

Seek out your support crew.

Remember, even if you work for yourself with no employees, you are not alone. Trying to do it all is not good for your mental health and doesn't make this pursuit much fun. Take a look around and seek out your support crew.

CREATING OPTIONS IS AT THE HEART OF YOUR SURVIVAL

The secret to survival could be in finding different ways to offer your services to suit different budgets during these turbulent times.

You may look at cutting up the services you offer - slicing off different parts to serve your (ideal) clients at varying price points. You could create a feeder product, a small product that is a step into your bigger products, or something with a lower price point that is 'easy to say yes to.'

As an example, if you are used to selling end-to-end strategic solutions, in the current market it's likely to be met with a conversation around, 'That's going to be hard to sign off.' Instead of thinking, 'Well this is what it costs, so I should walk away,' you could create a Business Health Check; a step before embarking on an end-to-end solution. This gives your potential client an understanding of how you think and a way to get to know your business (and vice versa), which may lead them to buying another stage in the process.

This approach empowers you to negotiate what you're worth, while considering a client's budgetary constraints, which is often a focus for clients in the current environment.

Your survival may depend on being able to take a flexible approach to the structure of your deals. By doing so, you will move the conversation away from, 'That's more than I wanted to spend.' towards, 'This is what we can achieve within your budget.'

What we can achieve within your budget.

PRICING UP PROJECTS

You've probably spent countless hours working out how to price up projects. Depending on how experienced you are in this significant part of business ownership, your approach to this may need some focus.

Being able to explain to a client why a project costs what it costs, involves knowing the effort required to deliver the promised result, coupled with having confidence in how you determined your base hourly rate in the first place.

There are many ways to charge clients for what you do. You may charge:

- by the hour,
- in blocks of hours,
- with a day rate,
- on a retainer,
- as a project fee, or
- something different.

If you typically work on longer term projects, let's explore a few ways you could shift your approach, so you are in a stronger position to negotiate your worth at the deals table.

CLIENT CHALLENGES AREN'T ALL UNIQUE

For several years as I met new clients, with new challenges, I kept thinking that each project and each client's solution had to be unique. I was wrong.

I would create bespoke solutions each time and spend a long time thinking about the best approach to each solution. What I later learned was that it's ok. In fact, it's better to have a framework and process that works for a specific type of client, with a specific problem.

There will absolutely be unique aspects in each project, however, the more problems you solve the more you can take a step back and look for patterns in what you're delivering.

Let's say you always give clients a checklist of information you want to review at the beginning of each project. Ponder if you do this for all clients or a good number of them. If this is the case, then you've got stage one of your framework – Information Gathering.

Look for the commonalities across your services and build products around those patterns.

This will give you confidence when negotiating with clients, as it will feel like familiar territory. When they ask you, 'How much might something like this cost?' you can give them a figure straight off the bat; a range (between xx or yy); or even a number of package options (package A, B or C).

This approach will give your clients comfort because they have a clear picture of what it will cost, and they can hear examples of similar projects you have delivered with comparable results.

But more importantly, it will give you confidence to ask for what you deserve to get paid for the work you do. It will empower you to say these numbers out loud without hesitation. And you will be able to determine if it works for your client, based on their verbal and physical reaction when you tell them the price.

TRACK YOUR DELIVERY TIME

Project charge-out rates can often feel like 'guess work' in the early days of business. Until you've got some experience under your belt and are starting to recognise patterns in your delivery, there are times when your quote may not match the time and effort you put in. This shift is to take into account all the time you spend on a project, on things that when you were *employed* were 'normal', but now you are a business owner often forget to add these into your fees. Things, such as time for WiP (work in progress) meetings and phone calls, all need to be considered in what we charge clients. Those of us who came from a 'regular' job often miss this, as we didn't need to consider it then.

And of course, each client's requirements will be a little different, but it's your business so you still want to be in the position to confidently answer the question, 'How much does something like that typically cost?'.

A little while into business ownership, there were a few types of projects that I really enjoyed working on and wanted to seek more of. I knew I could deliver great outcomes for my clients. Yet while I could articulate the value I could deliver, I didn't have a quick answer as to how much the project would cost them because, honestly, I didn't really know. If you're facing this situation, I suggest you start by carefully tracking your delivery time and effort.

The first step to shifting your ability to standardise your product is to track everything that is involved in delivering each project. Download a time tracking tool, start a spreadsheet, or just head a page in your note pad and note down every minute you spend on each and every task. Be specific, whether that be creating a document, conducting a WiP meeting, running a workshop... all of it.

I suggest doing this with 3-5 projects for the same service – by then you start to see patterns emerging; you will be able to use this data to see patterns in behaviour, in you and in your clients. Having this information will enable you to set a guide price for what the product typically costs, and how long it takes to deliver. You will have a definitive range in which to price the next similar project.

All this tracking gives you the ability to offer clients a guide price, as well as help them understand how long it takes, AND you can do all this expectation-setting without having to prepare a proposal, send it off, then wait.

For example, you can say, 'Based on what we've discussed, your best option is xxx product, which typically takes 6 weeks to deliver, and it will cost between xxx and yyyy. This will depend on how much your team are involved, or if you want my team to deliver everything. How does that sound?'.

BREAK YOUR WORK INTO PARTS

Take a step back to consider why clients invite us in to help solve their problems – the reality is, they don't really know how to solve these challenges themselves. If they did, they'd hire a temp rather than secure the services of a consultant. So, when you're proposing a solution, it's important to help clients understand what is involved in solving their problem.

When your work involves delivering large-scale solutions, it can be overwhelming for some clients to jump right in and sign off, especially those who haven't worked with you previously. So, if you can find ways to break down your work allowing them to buy 'pieces,' then you may find it easier to close the deal.

Potential clients want to understand the process you use to reach the outcome. Solutions can be offered in so many ways, and you will of course have your unique approach. If you can explain your approach as a series of stages, phases or modules, clients will be able to see the whole of what they are buying into. This will help them understand how you work, and it gives them confidence that you have a process (that they do not) and can deliver the results they are seeking.

The greatest advantage of breaking down your big projects into phases, is that you may be able to offer differing levels of support, that align with your client's budgets. Identify ways you could cut the pie, start with a small piece of work and then build into the delivery of the full program, over time.

Finding ways to package your products so you are easy to buy from, means people who haven't worked with you before may be able to 'test' the relationship with a less expensive product. This may be a Health Check process, a half day intro session, or executing stage one of a bigger project, followed by a review and agreement to proceed, or not.

Closing big deals takes longer than closing smaller ones, so taking a flexible approach may help you close more deals with ease.

WRAPPING IT UP

To endure tough times, embracing the BILBY's survival instincts will help you thrive.

Finding different ways to deliver your products embodies the true strength of smaller business. You can be flexible and move quickly if necessary, and breaking down what you do, makes it easier for your clients to buy.

Clearly articulating what you can do for your clients, removes fuzziness or ambiguity about the impact their investment will deliver.

Being a business owner can sometimes seem like a lonely pursuit but seek out your support crew so you know you're not alone.

All of this will make the tough times less stressful as you close deals with confidence. However, they may be deals of different shapes and sizes than you have been used to negotiating previously.

ACTION PLAN

What's the ONE action you'll take to harness your inner BILBY?

_____

PLATYPUS

Being sensitive to enable FLEXIBILITY

There's a great deal our quirky friend the Platypus can teach you about consistently negotiating good outcomes at the deals table. They are the world's only venomous furred animal but due to their hyper-sensitive powers they only throw their venom at times of high agitation.

For the most part, Platypuses keep to themselves, spending most of their day industriously foraging for food. Its sophisticated electromechanical system detects minute electrical signals given off by the muscles of its prey, which gives them an advantage in the survival stakes.

The Platypus is a symbol that you don't have to make a lot of noise to be powerful. Holding your power close and becoming more attuned and sensitive to environmental changes will help you survive and thrive as a business owner. Being sensitive to your environment increases your ability to forage for work that you enjoy, with clients you really want to work with.

Fundamentally, your success as a business owner is contingent on your ability to stand firm on your rates. However, you can't hold this power if you aren't sure how you came up with your rates in the first place, or where there is flexibility in them.

Not knowing your numbers means the whole process is set up for failure, with high levels of anxiety and stress – which may lead you to throwing some venom around when pushed hard by clients from time to time. For example, when a client asks something like, 'How did you come up with your rates?' you need to be sure of the answer instead of thinking: *'I don't know. It felt right. I think it's what you will pay.'* or other similarly fluffy responses. Picking a number out of *'I reckon'* thin air does not demonstrate your worth, nor support you being able to negotiate great outcomes for your business.

Feel free to ignore the rest of this whole book, but not this, this is it. Find a quiet spot, sit down, focus on the next few pages, and take action.

This chapter's outcomes will help you when being challenged to confidently say, 'I hear what you're saying about our fees, but there is no more flexibility in these numbers, they're in line with market rates and the number you're proposing is just not viable for my business. We might need to look at a different way to make this work or call it a day.'

Confidence in your numbers and pushing past cultural taboos to have some uncomfortable conversations is a must to securing a great result. This approach will enable you to be flexible when you sense it will have a positive impact on your enjoyment or deliver a long-term gain for your business. This will also save you a tonne of time and frustration, you should really start to enjoy the process with this in your burrow.

Let's step through a robust process for establishing your rates so you can unleash your inner Platypus powers.

MINDSET TIP

To help embrace this mindset, ponder these words from Tim Ferriss in his book *The 4-Hour Work Week*:

'A person's success in life can usually be measured by the number of uncomfortable conversations he or she is willing to have.

Nobody likes difficult conversations. They are stressful, emotionally charged, impossible to predict.

And because of that, it can be really tempting to try and avoid them.

That's what most people do, why shouldn't it work for us, too?

In fact, though, learning when and how to assert yourself and have an uncomfortable conversation is one of the most important social skills you can have – and will really benefit your overall quality of life.'

STEP 1. GOOGLE COMMON RATES

Doctor Google can help. In the following example, I have used the position of 'copywriter' but obviously apply the specifics to your service offering.

So, let's Google, 'What does a [copywriter] get paid per hour in [Australia]?' The results are typically prolific.

Invest an hour or three in reading through the results to get a good bank of knowledge to help you understand what a typical rate for a [copywriter] is.

Then ensure you put this in context: Are you a [junior or senior copywriter]? Are you a [generalist or technical writer]? There are many different parameters.

If you work across the world, search for this information in the countries where you work. Make sure you know if these countries call what you do by other names, then seek out that information too.

Consider where you would place your rates.

Once you have a bank of information, consider where you would place yourself and your rates relative to all of these benchmarks.

Knowing this will give you confidence in the value you bring to the table. If you're an experienced technical writer, for example, you're in a position to explain to a potential client where your fees sit in comparison to other less experienced, less specific copywriters. This will give them an understanding of your value, and invites them to do their own research, which will also give them confidence in your proposal.

STEP 2. RESEARCH YOUR COMPETITORS

A review of your current market environment can help contextualise your rates. Take a good look at who else is doing what you do. Understand who is delivering work to a similar standard as you, who isn't, and how they put their message to market, including information on their rates.

Note down the brands you know are your competitors. Return to Google and seek out a wider list of brands who are a similar size or smaller than you. Select some aspirational competitors too; these are bigger brands you would like to be pitching against.

Dedicate time getting to know what they do. Is what they're offering similar to your offering? Or learn how they differ. It might be in their products, processes, level of service, outputs, or something else, but ensure you understand it relative to your business niche.

In your investigation find out as much as possible about the organisation, their offering, and their team. Take a look at LinkedIn or similar sources to know more about their team's experience and how it's similar or different to yours.

Depending on your industry's norms, this next piece may take a bit more sleuthing. Find out if you can discover what rates they charge. With luck it will be on their website, or you may need to be a bit more creative.

Empowering you with the ability to benchmark your offering.

This activity is about gathering as much intelligence as possible, so you have a good understanding of who you may be pitching against. However, it's important not to get too bogged down in the detail. It's a learning exercise. It's about empowering you with the ability to benchmark your offering.

This information may be enough to give you more confidence moving forward and to believe in your product differentiators, along with the price you're putting to clients. It can also help you answer difficult questions like, 'Who else does what you do?'. You will be able to say, 'Company X does similar work, but they differ by [focusing on less bespoke solutions, which makes them cheaper].' This is another layer of confidence you can show to your potential clients that you know your worth and where you fit in the market.

STEP 3. IDENTIFY YOUR CAREER DIFFERENTIATORS

Consider what else you bring to the table. Many consultants have taken a variety of paths in their career to get to the role of business ownership. For example, while you may be working as a copywriter in your business now, you may have studied and practiced as a lawyer, or as a journalist, or as a marketer, in the past.

Let's say you were trained as a lawyer and are now a copywriter. While you're not going to promote that you can give legal advice, having this knowledge means you can suggest your clients seek legal advice if you see any legal red flags. This is valuable to a client and could potentially save them a great deal of pain and money down the track.

Look back over your career, think through what you're trained in, what skills you learnt on-the-job, and any other additional skills you bring to everything you do.

Think about how your previous experience can help your clients:

- save money,
- help them save time,
- reduce their risk, or
- deliver them greater value in some way.

Ensure you clearly weave that into your profile, website, and pitches to differentiate you from others. This will make it easier for them to choose to work with you, rather than your competitors.

STEP 4. COMPARE YOUR HOURLY RATE TO A SALARY

Outside of your competitors, another good source of rate comparison is a full-time employee's salary. Identify what your salary range would be if you were employed in another business. If you left a job to start your own business, offering a similar solution as you used to perform, this will be pretty straight-forward, as you have a salary rate to compare to.

If you didn't come from a similar role, it's time for more research. Check out job board websites, call a recruiter, and look up the Government Award Rate for your role and industry. You will need to be specific, as the salary for some roles varies dramatically from industry to industry. For example, a marketing co-ordinator in banking may get paid much more than one in a tech start-up, so ensure you get a good gauge on the range and how it compares to the target market for your business.

There are many ways to translate a salary to an hourly rate, and there are lots of conversion calculators online. Just type into your search engine: salary conversion calculators (in Australia).

Once you have this information, you can use it as a base to guide what your rates will be, or as another benchmark to confirm your initial thoughts. Depending on the complexity of the solutions you offer, you may charge hourly, daily or by project. All of these options are based on having clarity on your worth.

STEP 5. 'GUN FOR HIRE' RATE CONSIDERATIONS

If you have a specialised skill, that few organisations have a need to keep as a full-time position, you are probably viewed as a 'gun for hire'; someone engaged to solve a specific problem. As a premium service, this offering should attract a premium price tag, especially when compared to full-time employee rates. Everybody wins.

We are living in a transitional time when having a specific skill and having a full-time job are no longer mutually exclusive. Over recent years a significant shift has taken place. Smart organisations hire and use subject matter experts.

Commonly referred to as the Gig Economy, it's the process of solving problems by bringing together the best team from inside, or outside of an organisation.

It works well for all parties. An organisation can access your specialised skills to solve a specific challenge and execute the solution over a short period of time. While you get to focus on delivering what you do best, you also help them to quickly achieve their desired outcome, and you then move on to the next gig.

As a service-based business owner you are embracing the Gig Economy, offering a service that is essentially a 'gun for hire' to help others solve their URGENT and IMPORTANT challenges.

In the area that I work, it's rare for a brand to need more senior strategists. They usually have capable staff who can execute but lack the strategic direction to know where to concentrate their attention. So, bringing in an external consultant for a specific focus can be a great solution.

Securing your services for a specific purpose or project, usually on a relatively short-term basis, means organisations should be prepared to pay you a higher rate, compared to an employee's salary.

STEP 6. CREATE YOUR RATE CARD

With all the research you have gathered throughout this process, I recommend you now take the opportunity to create a rate card. Having a rate card arms you with a measured response when potential clients want to know, 'How much do your services typically cost?'.

To help you build this, you can complete the template that is **POWER TOOL 4**: **Create YOUR rate card.**

Business owners often say, 'Each client's requirements are different, so it's almost impossible to give them a guide price.' Another excuse I hear often is, 'I don't want to risk misquoting the job, so I usually go back and put together a proposal for the client and send it over on email.'

Ponder these questions for a minute:

- How uncomfortable do you feel when people ask you how much something costs, and you don't have an answer?

- How much time have you invested in writing up a proposal that did not go anywhere because when it got to the client it was way out of their budget expectations?

- How frustrating do *you* find it when someone can't give you a guide price on something you want to purchase?

Creating a rate card can resolve these *weird* conversations. When you give firm indicative pricing, it's important it comes from an educated place, even when you are clear that each client is different and what you share is just that – indicative. You can, of course, give them a range, 'between xxx and yyyy, depending on your business' specific requirements.'

Some people have different rates for services, even when the tasks are being delivered by the same person, but I find that a little challenging because it's all coming out of the same brain. However, if you're working with charities or other not-for-profit organisations, it's fair to say you will likely want to have a different rate compared to your for-profit clients.

Depending on the services or products your business offers, you may not have to publish or share your rates with your clients, however having a rate card provides a way to talk confidently at the deals table. You'll be in a strong position to:

1. Stand by your number, because you <u>know</u> how you came up with it.

2. Know how much you can flex on price, because you have built it sensitive to the client's you work with.

3. And you can calmly walk away from clients who do not align with your services and associated fees.

WRAPPING IT UP

With all this hard work under your belt, the next time a client says that annoying phrase, 'I can buy it from xxxx for half the price, why are your rates so high?' you are now in a position to help them understand the difference that working with your business will mean for them.

You should be able to explain why others charge less than you, and how it directly relates to the value they can expect from you in comparison.

You may even decide that some clients would be better suited to work with your competitors, and you can invite them to do so, rather than take a race to the bottom of the fee barrel.

You should now know exactly how to answer the question, 'How did you come up with your rates?'. That's not to say you won't get challenged - you will. And there is more work to be done on building in flexibility and different ways to price up work, but you should now be in a stronger, more confident position.

Like the PLATYPUS, protect yourself by ensuring you're armed with enough information so you aren't taken by surprise in a rate conversation with clients. No matter how shy or reserved you are, you can now hold your own at the deals table. You don't have to be loud to utilise your senses and stay aware of the shifting environments around you.

ACTION PLAN

What's the ONE action you'll take to harness your inner PLATYPUS?

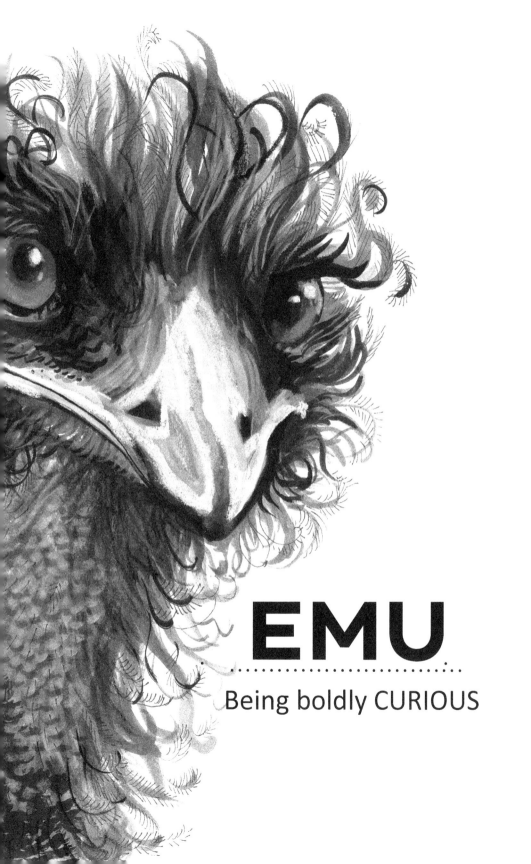

EMU

Being boldly CURIOUS

Old man Emu is a damn curious being. Standing at around two metres tall, Emus are naturally curious animals, they're a symbol of progress because they can't walk backwards easily, preferring to go forwards. They stick their beaks into places with great interest, walking forward to eyeball people with curiosity.

Just like our flightless friend, when you're negotiating your worth with a client, you prefer to go forwards, not backwards. You must continue onward, taking the lessons from each encounter, analysing the elements you want to build on, noting what went according to plan and recognising the steps in the process that made you feel powerful and in charge of your value.

And as you've learned so far in this book, your approach to the deals table *can* be made less stressful and more enjoyable by banking on some repeated patterns of behaviour from those you negotiate with regularly.

Build on this by pondering the Emu's curious ways – stand a little taller, be a little bolder. This will help you to be comfortable asking lots of questions, and to discuss money in spite of cultural taboos. Never shying away from an opportunity to explore the 'sticky bits' of a deal will empower you to continually make progress, no matter what setbacks you encounter.

If you can harness a bold and curious disposition, you will be able to enter any room and negotiate great outcomes.

Let's work through ways you can unlock your inner Emu powers.

INVEST IN YOUR PREPARATION

The bulk of your time should be spent preparing yourself to approach the deals table boldly and with curiosity, just like the Emu.

The good news is you've done much of the work already, as outlined in the other chapters of this book.

- You've investigated the behaviours of Your Ideal Clients.

- You've identified your response to the things they typically say in response to your articulation of your worth.

- You've spent time determining different ways to cut your products to align with current market behaviours.

Invest 70% of your time preparing for each negotiation.

I recommend you invest 70% of your time preparing for each negotiation. Yes, about 70% of the effort you expend for each deal is invested prior to entering the room. Depending on the importance of the negotiation, this may only take 5 minutes, or it could take a significant amount of time.

 To guide your thinking, complete your **PREPARE Cheat-Sheet,** which is part of the ***NEGOTIATION FUNDAMENTALS.***

This tool will guide your thinking. Being prepared, you'll enter the room with a clear mind. From previous patterns, you'll have recognised the questions that may arise, and you'll understand where you sit on different aspects of the deal.

With this approach, under your Emu feathers, you'll step up to the table ready to really listen to the other party. You'll be comfortable to discuss money when the time is right, as you have clarity on how you calculated your numbers, and you'll feel confident to stick your beak in and ask questions to satisfy your curiosity and discover if it's a good deal.

A BALANCED APPROACH –
DON'T WING IT, NOR OVER-PREPARE

Most people have one of two approaches to the deals table - they WING IT, or they CHOREOGRAPH IT.

Those who can think on their feet believe they can 'wing it' in any situation. However, being able to respond is one thing, but having responses that help you get consistently positive results at the deals table is another thing altogether.

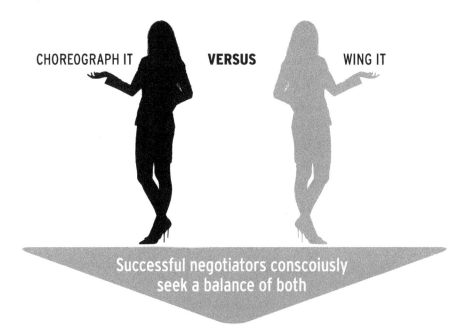

CHOREOGRAPH IT **VERSUS** WING IT

Successful negotiators conscoiusly seek a balance of both

When clients respond positively it feels easy for those who 'wing it,' but what if you're faced with someone who's a bit pushy? If you are challenged on your rates, you might find yourself getting frustrated or defensive.

When you haven't prepared the amount of anxiety you experience in the room can be surprising. Being under pressure to think on your feet can leave you wondering if you really did get the best deal.

On the flip side, those who 'choreograph it,' leave no stone unturned, preparing A LOT. Preparing what you want to say, assuming the conversation will go a certain way, hoping that it will go as you've laid it out.

If this is you, the spanner in the works comes when you enter the room and the discussion doesn't go how you imagine it. Having a tight script on how it will go, leads you to easily get thrown off course when it doesn't go that way. You can find yourself at a loss, your confidence fades, and you get disheartened that you didn't get what you went in to negotiate.

Annoyingly BOTH of these approaches cause anxiety. They can lead to the use of unhealthy, passive aggressive, or defensive language – and can cause a general sense of disappointment in yourself.

Be well prepared with flexibility built in.

The best option is to get a balance between the two. To consciously negotiate means to be well prepared with flexibility built in. If we do the heavy lifting prior to stepping in the room, we're calm. We've considered the situation from many different angles, so we can let the conversation flow. As a result, we're able to:

- think clearly,
- be creative,
- listen intently to the other person's position, and
- confidently participate in the negotiation.

WHERE TO POSITION YOURSELF IN THE ROOM

You may not be in the habit of being intentional about where you position yourself when you step up to the deals table, but this can have a big impact on your confidence.

Consider a time when you've entered someone else's office. They have a big mahogany desk and invite you to take a seat on the other side. This is an intimidating position. You may not realise it, but you are on the back foot here. In the 70's and 80's these big desks were intended to indicate power and position. While these office set-ups aren't commonplace these days, they still exist, and the person on the other side may still have that mindset.

Wherever possible, have discussions or negotiations on neutral territory. Try to get to the venue early and arrange the seating so it's an even playing field. Ideally you aren't on opposite sides, and if you have a team with you, get everyone to split up so it's not an 'us versus them' situation.

If you have no choice but to sit at the mahogany desk in their offices, move your seat so you are more beside the person than opposite. It's funny! My business is called Other Side of the Table, yet I try very hard to *never* sit on the opposite side of it.

Note, if you can't negotiate face-to-face ensure you do it via a video platform, rather than on the phone. This gives you the opportunity to eyeball the other party.

DON'T MAKE A PRE-EMPTIVE RUN

When threatened by predators, an Emu doesn't have the option to fly away. If attacked from above, they will cower down and run in a zigzag pattern; and they can run FAST - up to 50 kilometres per hour. However, up close their main defence is a swift kick with their powerful legs and sharp claws.

This is a reminder that you have options when you feel like the other party is pushing hard. If you've done all your preparation work, you should feel confident to stand your ground.

One thing to implement right now is to STOP negotiating over email. You may think it's easier to have a nice chat face to face, go back to your desk and send a proposal through, then close your eyes, cross your fingers, and wait - but it isn't.

STOP negotiating over email.

I get it, most people don't feel comfortable talking about money, but it can be costing you a huge opportunity to grow your business and build your confidence. You've started zigzagging before a threat has even presented itself - a pre-emptive run.

Negotiating by email is dangerous. It's impersonal, and you will miss opportunities to read the other person's body language, or to work *together* to explore a way forward. It doesn't give you the chance to land a powerful kick that could reach an agreement quickly.

You also give them an opportunity to lock you out with a few strokes of the keyboard. It's really easy for them to say, 'Thanks, but no thanks.' and shut the door on the discussion. Come on, this is Sales 101 - don't box yourself in by negotiating via email.

WHEN SHOULD YOU TALK TO CLIENTS ABOUT MONEY?

Most of us have been raised in a society where talking about money is discouraged, so it makes us uncomfortable. There are so many taboos and negative conversations to demonstrate this, including 'It's rude to discuss what you earn with others.' We can't ask how much something costs as, 'That would be rude.' too.

However, as a business owner your primary job is to bring in the money. So, it's time to get comfortable with the uncomfortable conversations. If you continue to let negotiations *happen to* you, rather than fully participate in them, then it's likely you will always leave something on the table.

Instead, build it into **YOUR Negotiator Language Bank** and, over time, you will learn to confidently talk about money.

Take your head out of the sand, and start talking about money ANY TIME YOU CAN, as early as possible, not only in business negotiations, but in other parts of your life. Do this until it becomes part of what you do, and you're ok with it.

Take any opportunity to discuss what you charge with potential clients, other business owners, and your business coach. By baking it into the way you do business you will start to look forward to these conversations. Ensure it's on your cheat sheet and use it to prepare for each interaction with your clients. Then say it loud and proud!

Remember you don't want to waste your time with people who can't afford you. As you become more confident, you can start discussing costs in the first phone call with potential clients. This can simply be done by asking, 'What's your budget expectation?' If they don't know, you can talk about your fees and how they are structured.

MINDSET TIP

To help understand this mindset, consider Stephen Covey's (author of *The Seven Habits of Highly Effective People*) perspective:

"People with a scarcity mentality tend to see everything in terms of win-lose. There is only so much; and if someone else has it, that means there will be less for me. The more principle-centered we become, the more we develop an abundance mentality, the more we are genuinely happy for the successes, well-being, achievements, recognition, and good fortune of other people. We believe their success adds to...rather than detracts from... our lives."

Everyone wants a good deal, but it's important that your client getting a good deal is not at the expense of you getting paid what you deserve.

'AM I ALLOWED TO ASK THAT?'

Another hiccup in your progress towards empowered deal negotiating, is when you have important questions you just don't ask.

If your potential client is using lots of jargon, or is not being clear on what they want, or what their budget is, you really must ask for clarification. But there may be times when you feel like, 'I don't really know what they mean by that, but I'll look stupid if I ask more questions.' Or, you're thinking, 'I wonder what their budget is, but it would probably be overstepping if I asked that.'

STOP that. Stick your beak in and eyeball your client. Be CURIOUS. You can never ask too many questions!

Say those things out loud; get comfortable asking the uncomfortable questions. That way you won't be left scratching your head, sitting at your desk trying to write a scope of work with the burden of trying to figure it out alone. You need to ask the questions that allow you to make the best decision for your business.

Some of the work I do is to support leaders as an integrated part of their team on game-changer deal negotiations. These deals are the ones that can significantly impact their business, positively or negatively, depending on the outcome. This 'tactical response' support may involve: working with a business owner whose company is being acquired; someone negotiating the terms of a preferred supplier deal; or supporting a senior leader learning to negotiate different outcomes with challenging personalities.

As you can imagine, there is a lot of strategy and planning invested in these deals. We spend significant time planning out how it might go, considering who might say what, and role-playing what we will do, say, or ask when that happens. No matter how long I do this job, it fascinates (and frightens) me that, during this preparation, so many leaders ask, 'Am I allowed to say that?' or 'Can I ask that?'.

Absolutely!!!! If you're not the one asking it, who will? You <u>are</u> the boss, so you <u>can</u> ask whatever you want.

It's important to find your voice and give the words oxygen, rather than kick yourself later wishing you had taken a deep breath and asked the tough questions. There's a ton of questions you might find yourself shying away from, but here are some examples:

- What does that acronym stand for?
- What's your budget?
- Do you have conflicting priorities for this spend?
- Is it the best time to roll out this project?
- How did you come up with how much you thought it might cost?
- What's your expectation on the level of seniority of the staff you want on this project?
- How would you approach this if you were me?
- Would you accept those terms if you were on this side of the table?
- I haven't come with a fully formed proposal. Shall we co-create the solution?
- Do you see us continuing to work together once this project is complete?

By asking more questions everyone wins you learn what they truly mean, and in turn, they feel heard. If you shy away from asking questions or having tough conversations, you're really fostering a relationship of 'us' and 'them.' But, if you push past the discomfort and ask what you really need to know, it becomes more and more about 'us,' 'we,' 'together we can...'. It's a great way to quickly build a sense of team, trust, and rapport.

There are many sites, blogs, and books that can give you additional information about the best ways to ask questions, but in my experience be mindful to ask open questions, the who, how, what, why, when, how much. These questions will assist you to progress the conversation. If, at the end of the conversation, you have to say no, at least you have explored the options fully and can make an informed decision.

YOU CAN HANDLE 15 SECONDS OF PAIN

As discussed above, you should not have to guess what a client means or what they want. If they aren't being clear, you don't have to gain permission to ask a question that seeks clarification to make an informed decision to say yes or no to the work.

You don't have to rush, and you don't have to have all the answers on the spot, BUT you do need to get the words out of your mouth, so it can become a discussion in the first place.

Getting the words from inside your head, past the (loud) beating of your nervous heart, and out of your mouth into the air, can all be done with less than 15 seconds of pain.

Next time you're in a meeting and think about something but hesitate... STOP. Write down what you want to say. If you have an extra moment, think:

- What's the worst thing that could happen?
- Could it simply open up the conversation?
- What might they say in response?
- What's the best thing that could happen?

Say it out loud, then don't say anything for 15 seconds. Shhhh. Wait for them to process what you've said, ponder it, then respond.

This process is what I call the 15 seconds of pain.

That's all it takes.

The awkward 15 seconds where you are waiting for them to respond but are dying to jump in and fill the silence.

Say it out loud, then don't say anything for 15 seconds. Shhhh.

It hurts for such a very short amount of time, but this will help you become stronger and bolder at every deals table.

The risk of not stepping up and asking the right questions can be enormous for you and your business. There may be ambiguity left in the room, which can often extend the negotiation, or end with the client taking advantage of your silence. You may find yourself agreeing to a deal that doesn't align with your revenue margins. Or you end up agreeing to work that doesn't truly fall into your product suite or ideal client profile. You might simply end up agreeing to a deal that isn't in the best interest for your business.

Having the conversation in the room will be hard, and for 15 seconds you will want the world to swallow you up, but over time this will become less and less stressful. AND you will save yourself a bunch of time not writing up proposals that come to nothing, or with terms you aren't happy with.

Remember though, if you still require clarity, and didn't ask a necessary question at the time of the negotiation, it's ok to ask later. You can always follow up with a call to say, 'I've been thinking about our chat, and I should have asked [x, y, z]. Can you please clarify [a, b, c]?'

To help you stay curious throughout the twists and turns of negotiations refer to the **POWER TOOL 5: Keep YOUR Curiosity in Negotiations.**

CAN YOU TAKE THE STING OUT OF ASKING FOR A BIG NUMBER?

When you work on big projects, they naturally have big numbers attached to them. In turn, it's natural for clients to have a reaction to these numbers, regardless of the expectation, so you should be aware that you may receive an 'initial' adverse reaction. The more often you talk about money, the more comfortable you will be saying the big numbers, however the initial reactions are always likely to be there.

MINDSET TIP

To help embrace this mindset, consider author, spiritual leader, and political activist, Marianne Williamson's thoughts on the money conversation:

"In the area of work and money, we have one of the most intense gaps between fear-based and love-based thought. It's not that a miracle mindset applies to work and money any more than it applies to anything else; rather, it applies there no less than anywhere else."

It's important that as you lay out your solution, you do so in a way that gives a clear understanding of how long it will take to roll out and what's involved in each part of the process. It should also enable you to explain why it will cost between xxx and yyy.

Giving clients a clear picture of what's involved and adding a detailed explanation around milestones or success metrics, will give them assurance of the value you are able to deliver.

If they say, 'Well that's more than I thought it would cost.' you may like to ask them questions around their expectations. Questions posed as:

- How much did you think it might cost and what was that based on?

- This pricing is based on our experience delivering similar projects. Would you like to see a case study of the results from one or two of these clients?

- There is a great deal involved in this project. Perhaps the solution I'm suggesting is more comprehensive than you require. Shall we go back over what's involved so we can confirm what I heard is aligned with your outcome expectations?

- I appreciate other companies charge less for less comprehensive solutions. Would you like to obtain some comparable quotes before we proceed?

Instead of being taken aback by your client's pain when hearing the price, this approach is about moving forward through it, so you can help them understand how you have determined your rates and show them you are open to scrutiny. They want to know this is a good investment for their business so being curious and open to their questions builds their confidence in your abilities.

If they don't see the value then perhaps this project isn't their biggest priority at this time, or they may just be looking for a cheaper solution.

WHAT'S IN OR OUT OF THE BUCKET?

It you've invested the effort and are clear on your calculated rates and value, when a client asks, 'Is that price negotiable?' you should be in a position to say, 'Absolutely, what would you like to take out of the bucket so we can make it work with your budget?'.

Any reasonable budget can be worked to.

That may not be the first words that spring to mind, but hopefully you get the point that any reasonable budget can be worked to, while representing value to both parties. You don't need to discount your worth to fit someone else's purse.

You can offer a range of responses from *YOUR Negotiator Language Bank*. Things such as:

- 'Perhaps we can stage the roll out for this project.'
- 'What if we ran a pilot to test it first?'
- 'I'm happy to work with your budget. We'll just have to take some elements out of the bucket, to be able to meet that.'
- 'Perhaps this isn't the right time for this project – if your budget is conflicted, let's push this back 3 months and I'll get in touch then.'

If you are clear on what's involved in delivering the promised outcomes, you will be able to push back at the deals table.

WHAT ARE YOU FOCUSING ON?

When you're in the room you may be focusing on the wrong thing. If you view these situations as a series of conversations, you can break them down as such:

- First session to set the scene and get a picture from each side.
- Subsequent session to discuss particular parts of the deal where you don't agree.

This approach helps to reduce stress and save time, especially for complex negotiations. Instead of focusing on the negotiation as a whole:

- break it down into parts,
- identify what really matters to either party, and
- discuss the sticking points.

This bottom-up approach will make it less painful to reach agreement, or to agree it's not going to work, and you have to walk away.

WRAPPING IT UP

The topics outlined in this EMU chapter are probably the most challenging of all the content in this book, so you may want to labour on these pages and work through it in partnership with your business coach.

These changes will take time, they will require you to be curious, be critical, and embrace your growth mindset – but they will have many aspects to their return on effort for a long time to come.

So remember, stand in your power and embrace old man EMU by looking at ways to always move forward. Learn from what you do and bolster *YOUR Negotiator Language Bank*.

Being comfortable to step up, stick your head in and be curious about the humans that sit before you, will help you feel more and more comfortable to ask for what you deserve.

ACTION PLAN

What's the ONE action you'll take to harness your inner EMU?

BIG RED
KANGAROO

·····································

TRAILBLAZING your path

The powerful big Red Kangaroo is an Aussie icon, a symbol of strength and power, and a trailblazer. They survive in our expansive outback, leading their mob, forging a path that keeps them thriving.

They explore vast areas of unchartered territory, as efficiently as possible, while making decisions on when to turn-tail and run for their survival.

When you're forging your own path as a business owner, you constantly have to make decisions that affect your survival. Others are likely relying on your capabilities, and your bravery. While there is risk in this pursuit, not making the tough calls ends up costing more in the long run.

There will be times when you'll have to turn-tail and run. This is not a negative, it's about survival. Your business is more likely to survive if you're working with people you can do your best work with, because you're enjoying yourself. Your sanity can also benefit from being more conservative with where you focus your energy.

Let's explore aspects to unlocking your inner big Red Kangaroo's powers.

In the early stages of business ownership, when you're working hard to get business in the door, you can learn so much from the people you encounter, their responses to what you offer, and how you have valued that. This information can be really helpful to shape your products, inform your marketing and sales messages, and validate your value.

Sadly though, in my experience, some reactions from potential clients can be downright rude. They come from an uninformed place. They say things like, 'I don't know where you got your pricing from, but that's just way out of my budget!'.

At the time I didn't hear what he was really saying to me. I thought I had my pricing all wrong. That was not, in fact, the case, as all this client wanted was a cheap solution. He was not my ideal client, and I should have walked away immediately, but unfortunately I didn't. Instead I agreed to a lower rate AND spent the entire time trying to demonstrate I was worth every cent, even though he was never going to find the real value in what I offered. Aghhhh, that was an exhausting and depressing experience.

On the upside, I am glad I experienced a wide range of rejections, so I had a benchmark to refine the clients I really enjoy and respect the opportunity to work with.

MINDSET TIP

To help embrace this mindset, consider motivational speaker and author Brian Tracy's thought:

"The more you focus on the value of your product or service, the less important the price becomes."

These experiences have helped me understand that while I want to eat, there are just some clients I do not want to, and will not work with, no matter how tough the market gets. There are people who do not align with my ideal client profile and come along every now and again to distract me with a challenge or a shiny opportunity. In hindsight, I now know I would rather suffer through home-brand beans for a month, than work with someone who just doesn't 'get it' (and I loathe baked beans by the way!). To do this, I've had to stand tall like my strong and powerful mate, old Red, and have some uncomfortable conversations declining opportunities that do not serve me, but it's been better than the alternative.

In the vast land of exploring new business, there is a lot of ground to cover; there are plenty of potential clients and projects out there. But the truth is, we are not the right option for everyone, and everyone isn't right for us. There will be times that you will need to make a tough choice, but it gets easier as you learn when you need to walk away.

We are not the right option for everyone.

SURVIVAL THROUGH CONSCIOUS DECISIONS

During challenging times, you will be making decisions very differently than when the economy is humming. You may at times consciously decide to take on work you don't love, with people who don't fit your ideal client. However, at these times, you will be choosing to make the decisions needed to survive.

When I look at the work my team and I have delivered in 2020, it was work we could do and we're good at - it just didn't light us up. I made some decisions based on the work that was available; it may not always be the work we love 100%, but I accepted some short-term pain, so that we could make it through the challenging year.

It may not be the kind of work that is inspiring, well paid, or playing completely to our strengths, but it kept the business going. The key to succeeding has been to remind ourselves that we agreed to the work for our survival.

That is an entirely different situation than when you go against your gut and unconsciously take on a project that doesn't align with your ideal client profile. We've all done it. I know when I find myself not enjoying the work I'm doing I ponder why I'm not having fun, then step back and think, 'Damn, I've done it again, I've taken on a project from someone that doesn't align with our ideal client profile.'

This can happen for many types of reasons. For example:

- You're excited about the process of closing a deal;
- You may be having a slow month and think, 'We have time, so why not squeeze it in'; or
- Despite the client wanting you do the work at much lower rates than you deserve, your people-pleaser gene has kicked in and you just accept it, rather than walk away.

Let's take a look at the indicators that might help you identify when you should consider walking away from a deal, earlier rather than later.

To help you easily identify when it's time to exit a negotiation, refer to the **POWER TOOL 6: When it's YOUR time to Turn Tail.**

TRUST YOUR GUT

When your gut instinct tells you that this is going to end badly, you should probably listen. If you've ever spent any time observing a Kangaroo, you'll notice they look like they are pondering what's going on around them. They'll be standing tall, chewing on a bit of grass, and seemingly taking it all in. The next thing you know, they're off. The rest of the mob turn tail too and everyone is on the move.

They sense when something isn't right. They may not know what, but the beauty is in the fact that they don't question it, they just head on down the road.

'I knew it wasn't right from the start!'

Think back to a time when you took on a project that ended badly. As you reflect on this, do you recall having a 'funny feeling' early on that it wasn't going to end well? Was there something about the other team's approach that 'didn't sit right'?

Instead of turning tail, you squashed the thought and kept pushing ahead. It was only later you realised, 'Damn, I knew it wasn't right from the start!'.

I have done this many times. In the early days I was so focussed on my desire to survive, that I ignored my gut's ability to help me identify times when I should leg-it! I remember saying yes to one particular project, despite knowing something was off. I just couldn't put my finger on the problems, but I also wasn't brave enough to ask the right questions, to be clear on everyone expectations.

As I worked my way through the project, it became very evident the Project Brief they had prepared didn't align with the full requirements and involved a lot more work than I expected – and a LOT more than had been budgeted for in my response. After over-servicing the deal for a while, I decided I'd had enough and had to say something.

'US' and 'THEM' view of consultants.

When I explained the situation with the project lead, he pushed back pretty hard, telling me I should have picked this up earlier, and the budget was fixed so, 'kinda too bad.' I was so shocked. I didn't know what to say, BUT, on reflection that night I remembered the feeling I had that something was off from day one. The feeling was he had an 'US' and 'THEM' view of consultants, rather than a 'we're all in this together' approach that I prefer. I set about finding a way to exit stage left, as soon as possible.

If you know your gut instinct is a good guide for your decisions, slow down and take its opinion into consideration from now on. There's nothing to lose by backing away and reconsidering your position. You can always re-engage down the track.

EFFORT VERSUS REWARD

Every piece of work needs to deliver a fair exchange in value for the effort that you will expend in delivering it, so ensure each project makes economic sense for your business.

Let's say you've met with a client and you've taken a project brief. During the discussion they were clear on what they wanted as outputs and were also very clear they had a fixed budget with no wiggle room.

As you've delivered similar projects like this many times, you know that no matter how you cut the deal, it feels like their expectations and their budget don't align.

It's now up to you to decide, if you:

- Explain that the amount of effort typically required for a project like this is significantly higher than they are predicting, citing examples from past clients to give them confidence in you.

- Let them know you can work to their budget, however, you're not going to be able to deliver all their desired outcomes, so you ask if they are open to a staged approach to the roll out, (refer to the section about, *What's in and out of the bucket?*)

- Take the work under their terms anyway, because you can see the money on the table, even though right here, right now, you know it's not going to be worth it for your business – the effort versus the reward doesn't stack up.

As a leader, you need to decide where to focus your collective efforts. Your survival and ability to grow depend on where you choose to best expend your energy. When your currency is grazing on paddocks with low levels of grassland versus guiding your mob down the road to find another more prosperous paddock, everyone is looking to you to make the call.

I hear my CFO's voice in the back of mind saying 'all deals need to work;' they need to stack up for everyone. In a service-based business it's easy to think, 'Well I'm not busy, and it's only my time which doesn't cost me anything.'

IT DOES!! Your time IS valuable.

Walk away, rather than get stuck with a dud deal.

Why agree to be paid a pittance for your valuable work? You could be sitting on the sofa binging the latest hit show, OR in the park spending time with your kids making priceless memories. It's time to think differently about how you value your time. This will positively impact when you are at a crossroad deciding to stay or go.

If a deal can't work, it can't work. Walk away, rather than get stuck with a dud deal for your business. A few minutes in an uncomfortable conversion will pay dividends for you in the long run.

WHEN IT FEELS TOO HARD

'WOW, you're very expensive.' Ahhh, one of my favourite lines from someone I now know is about to become an ex-prospect.

I once got told, 'You charge as much as a brain surgeon!'. Looking back, especially with what I charged then, I know he was completely out of touch with reality. We had a misalignment in value that was never going to come together. He was seeking a cheap solution, and his commentary was more a sign that he would never see value in what I would deliver for his business. Oh well... See ya!

Sadly, it didn't go like that, I didn't walk away. I was hungry and wanted the work. I took his statement as my opportunity to change his mind, but I metaphorically went 'round after round' with this client. It turned out it didn't really matter what number I put on the table; it just wasn't low enough for him.

In the next round of the (brutal) negotiations, I moved from offering brain surgeon rates to that of a General Practitioner. And so it went on – he wanted the bucket, its contents, and my right kidney.

I didn't enjoy the work. I didn't enjoy his consistent jabs about my rates. And my confidence was shaken. The only thing I was excited about was when the job was done, I could leave and never speak to him again.

I wish I'd seen the signs from the get-go. If someone treats you like that in the negotiation stage, it is a clear indicator of what it will be like to work with them. 'Start as you mean to go on.'

When someone is pushing too hard on the price, walk away.

So, please learn from my three rounds of suffering on fee value. When someone is pushing too hard on the price, walk away, say thanks but no thanks, say, 'perhaps now isn't the right time for this project.' Get out. Don't stay in the ring; the hits hurt (your confidence).

Speaking of rounds in the ring, our mate Big Red wouldn't take that. He'd lean back and box it out, then stand over the top as the victor so his opponent would never forget him. I don't recommend this approach, but you can embrace his power when you are facing an unreasonable foe.

MAYBE YOU'RE NOT RIGHT FOR THIS

Sometimes people come to you with a job, and you think, 'Did this person actually read my website? Because what they're asking me to do, is nothing like what I actually do.'

It's funny, but the next thought that often comes over you is, 'Oh well, I'm sure I can Google how to do this.'

And by the time they finish the overview of what they need and say, 'Is that something you can help us with?' you don't flinch and respond with something like, 'Totally, I'm happy to help!'.

Either that, or someone asks you to do a task that you're very capable of delivering but you just don't enjoy and don't want to do, but you respond in the same way, 'Yep, I can do that.' because you feel sick at the thought of giving away work, *just in case* it leads to something more meaty or more interesting that's actually in your wheelhouse.

Well, you'll be pleased to know, there definitely comes a time when you have the luxury of admitting that you really aren't the best person for the job. That sickening feeling disappears as you recommend someone you know is more suitable or qualified for what they require, or even someone who will enjoy it more than you. By being selective, it shows a level of maturity that people respect, and through this process you may find people you can collaborate with on bigger projects.

WRAPPING IT UP

By embodying the characteristics of the big RED KANGAROO, you'll puff your chest out, stand as tall as you're able, and face the fact that you are talking to the wrong person. This is not a client for you. Instead, turn tail and explore where you will find your Ideal Client.

Without this focus, being rejected or interrogated by someone who's not a good match for you, can lead to a loss of confidence. They don't understand your value because they're not the right person to work with; they're looking for something or someone else.

Determining your business will be better off for having these challenging conversations, will pay off in the long run. Knowing when to walk away, or to move in a different direction, will ensure your survival and keep you standing in your power.

Look for the signs, listen to what people are really saying from the day you meet them, and position yourself to know early if they don't align with your business.

ACTION PLAN

What's the ONE action you'll take to harness your inner big RED KANGAROO?

_____

WOMBAT

Being clear on your BOUNDARIES

With their strong, stocky build, a koala-like nose and a low-slung belly, the Wombat is one of Australia's most memorable animals. Despite their appearance they can run, quickly! In fact, they could give Usain Bolt a run for his money in line with his Olympic sprint record, having recorded speeds of up to 40 kilometres an hour.

Like so many native Australian animals, Wombats are just so loveable, but they can be underestimated. They have a raft of hidden talents; the most relevant to supporting your quest, is their ability to set strong boundaries. To do this, the Common Wombat, also known as the Bare-nosed Wombat, marks the perimeter of their territory with their unmistakable, square-shaped poop.

Now, I'm not suggesting you start marking your territory, instead let's focus on your ability to be clear about your boundaries; embracing your role in saying 'no' when things don't align with your values. You can learn to be firm in the negotiation room and say 'no' when a deal isn't right.

As the boss, it's your job to say no when a deal is not good for your business. If you work in an organisation with shareholders or a Board, there would be expectations on you to make sound financial decisions. However, many people who run their own business don't have someone to answer to, so this rigour can be sporadic or absent.

Consider your discussions with clients and the rates you charge them. Imagine you have a Board; what would they say about your revenue decisions? There may be no one 'watching,' but it's likely, if you're shying away from fee negotiations or agreeing to slash your proposed pricing, you are compromising your worth.

For every hour you work at a reduced rate, you will be negatively impacting your self-belief in your ability and what you're worth.

This is NOT on the client - this is on YOU.

Finding your voice to say no will have a HUGE impact on you and your business goals, not to mention your bottom line.

Let's look at a few ways you can find your voice and learn to embrace your inner Wombat, empowering you to, 'Say NO like a BOSS'.

IS YOUR 'PEOPLE-PLEASER' GENE IMPACTING YOUR SUCCESS?

You're the boss of a revenue generating organisation, so you have to find a way to stop wanting to please everyone. The reality is, if you are worried about everyone's 'feelings' and linking their approval to your worth, you are going to lose confidence, which will lead to lost revenue.

Changing this is likely to be a challenge, however, it is possibly one of your biggest handbrakes to success.

Ask yourself, 'Why are you trying to please *everyone*?'. If you do a good job and deliver outstanding work, isn't that enough?

If you're pleasing everyone, shouldn't that include pleasing yourself and your business? When you're running a commercial entity, your first obligation needs to be to your mental health, then to the bottom line of your business.

If you are linking your success to a client's approval of a scope of work, you will probably be chipping away at the value you can deliver by reducing your rates until your client is happy. People pleasers can leave lots of money on the table like this, when they really need to focus on pleasing their own bottom line.

MINDSET TIP

To help embrace this mindset, consider Brené Brown's (professor and author) perspective on being a people pleaser:

"One of the most painfully inauthentic ways we show up in our lives sometimes is saying 'yes' when we mean 'no,' and saying 'no' when we mean 'hell yes.'

Part of the challenge here is that, as we are in the business of selling our intelligence, we can forget to value every minute we take our butts off the sofa, or away from our family, or off the ski fields. How much is your time really worth?

Saying no has a great deal of guilt associated with it, especially for people-pleasers. It feels like we're letting the other person down or exposing a weakness in our capability. But it shouldn't be that way. Your ability to say no reflects the power your hold over your own worth.

DO YOU SAY YES WHEN YOU MEAN NO?

Think of the times when you've said yes to a project, but you knew you should have said no. Think how often that happens. If you are regularly agreeing to fees you know are too low because you don't have the right language in your pouch to say no with confidence, then STOP IT.

You're damaging your confidence, your reputation and your business.

Stop it, because you're damaging your confidence, your reputation, and your business. If you accepted the terms of the deal, and you said yes when you should have said no, the result will be having to deliver a project for less than you are worth.

Once you come to terms with that, your natural instinct may be to start the next negotiation by telling them how they got an outstanding deal the first time, and they should expect a significant rate hike on any future deal.

It might surprise you to hear that this is classic passive-aggressive behaviour. What it *sounds* like you're saying, is that you feel they took advantage of you. There's a risk they may think, 'Oh, they don't always say what they mean, so can I trust them?'.

Don't overthink this though, you're not an island - this is an Aussie specialty. We do it in lots of situations and it's typically because we don't like to disappoint people or let people down because we're not used to engaging in the uncomfortable conversations. We say yes when we really mean no. It's done with the best of intentions, however, whilst we don't mean to lie to people, when it comes to light months, or even years later, it can really hurt, everyone.

Let me give you a personal example. A few years ago, I rang one of my favourite people and asked if I could come and stay with a couple of friends who were travelling. She said, 'Of course, and excitingly we have a ton of people coming over that weekend, so you'll all be able to enjoy the festivities!'. Wonderful! I told my international guests we were a go, everyone booked flights, happy days. We enjoyed a fabulous stay, a great celebration, and new friends were made all around.

All good, until two years later when this person was telling someone else the story about how, 'Sammy came to stay with two friends on the busiest weekend of the year, when we were hosting a ton of people at our house.'

When I heard her tell the story like that I was gutted. After some time of reflection, it was obvious that she had said yes, when she really meant no. I had no idea, but in hindsight I felt terrible, and a little part of me wondered what else she says yes to when she doesn't mean it?

I share this story, as an out-of-context example of the impact of kicking the can down the road and dealing with an awkward conversation. By saying no when you mean no, you prevent this situation arising. It's better for your reputation in the long term, to push through uncomfortable conversations and say what you really mean.

You need to learn how to rip off the band-aid, and just say, 'Look this doesn't work for me – it's not a good time.' or, 'It's not a sound business decision – you understand, right?' .

When I've had to renegotiate deals with clients who got 'newbie' business owner rates, or deals I've given low rates thinking there was a bigger deal over the hill, I've been up front with them. I've come at it with some curiosity, letting them know with something like, "You appreciate those rates are 'introductory rates,' and far below my normal market rate." And later when negotiating the next deal, 'Now we've been here for a while, I'm sorry to tell you that we're going to have to look at shifting the rates we gave you to align more with current market rates.' This approach opens up the discussion and gets the rates moving upwards. If you're going in with low rates, let them know upfront that they are getting a 'special' deal....and put it in writing.

However, to shift away from this behaviour forever, take a leaf out of the Wombat's playbook: slow down, take a lap of the perimeter, re-mark your boundary. While taking this virtual walk around the block, take stock of what's important to you. Don't rush back to the deals table. Be introspective and know the worth of what you deliver to your clients.

THE BEST THING ABOUT 'NO' – 'NO' HAS MANY FRIENDS!

Where no is concerned, we're challenging another taboo – saying no to someone doesn't mean you can't be polite. Just because it's a no from you, doesn't mean you're being rude in order for you to do what's right for you or your bottom line. And the best thing about no, is that it's friends with great words including: no but; no and; no not now; as well as, no thank you.

If reading these few statements makes you think 'That's all good in theory, but I can't see a world where I say no a lot,' well, you're reading the right book to change all that; you CAN do this, you WILL do this. It might not happen straight away, but one day in the future you will feel empowered to say no as many times as is required – and as you'll be saying no in a way that works for you, it'll feel natural, and it will be an indicator that your business is really hum.

I've known some people who opt to do silly things like triple their rates rather than have an uncomfortable conversation, when they don't want to work with a particular client.

But if someone is not treating you right, you may not be the first person they've tried to engage to solve their problem. They are likely to be the ones to say yes to a crazy rate because they're just happy to find someone who will work with them. Then it will be you who has to work with them!! I do not recommend this. Instead, be up front and just say no.

5 WAYS TO SAY NO

Saying no is not personal; you're saying no to the opportunity, not to the person.

How you say no is also important. There are countless ways to do this, but to help get you in the habit of saying it out loud, here are five ways to say no:

1. No, but…

I think I know a way we might be able to make this work. If we stage the approach to this deal….

2. No, thank you…

Perhaps I'm not the right supplier for your challenge. I could recommend an alternative supplier who delivers good work to lower specs and budgets…

3. No, and…

It's been interesting chatting to you, but I'm not the right person to help you. Based on what you've said, you may need to rethink your project. Perhaps [insert a completely different provider] would be in a better position to solve your problem…

4. No, maybe…

It might not be the right time for this project, as it sounds like your budget is conflicted. Maybe we should revisit this project in a few months' time….

5. No.

I'm sure you can appreciate I have to decline this opportunity, as the current terms of the deal are unviable for my business to accept.

DEPERSONALISE THE CONVERSATION

Emotions can run high when we are saying no to any opportunity. In 'I Love Negotiating,' I talked about your choice of language in a negotiation. It's important to be mindful that nothing in this situation is personal – it's business. In fact, you should specifically aim to depersonalise a negotiation.

Choosing specific language when describing your position can help with this. It takes practise, but it makes a major difference.

Consider a particularly sensitive subject, such as negotiating your salary with your manager. You need to depersonalise your vocabulary as much as you can.

1. Replace 'you' with 'the company'. It's not your manager that decides the rules, it's the company. You want your manager to be your advocate, so it's important that you appreciate their position. When you're saying 'you haven't done this or that' it makes it personal, and it may put them on the back foot.

2. Next, swap 'me' with 'someone in my position'. You are asking for a pay rise because someone in your position – i.e. someone being asked to put in the hours, manage the staff, or deliver on certain KPIs – would expect to be remunerated in the way that you are suggesting. Your pay grade is not a privilege, it is an exchange of value (your effort for a good day's pay).

3. Finally, consider changing 'I believe' with 'a reasonable person would think/do/act' in this situation. This simple twist will reduce the risk that the other person feels you are blaming them. Your goal is to separate the people from the problem; to remove the personal passion from the conversation. This is one of the most effective methods of defusing a tense situation, but also a very difficult habit to get into – so practise it today.

It's important that it's not about 'YOU' and 'ME,' but more about what is fair and is a reasonable exchange in value.

To be successful in saying NO Like A Boss, you must decouple yourself from the outcome. Negotiations become messy if we make them personal, so make a commitment to not do that.

To help you with what can be uncomfortable moments, invest some time to populate the **Power Tool 7: Articulate YOUR Boundaries.**

THIS ISN'T WORKING, LET'S DISCUSS.

There will be times when you've already said yes to a deal, yet while you're executing the project you find yourself getting frustrated. Perhaps you're feeling annoyed with doing the work or finding requests from the client are outside what was initially discussed. Perhaps when you take a step back, you realise they are being unreasonable with what they are asking. During these times it's important to take a moment to reassess the terms of the deal you negotiated.

This is not a time to shy away from having an open conversation with your client. Big projects can roll out differently than anticipated during the building of the scope of work. You may end up working on a wider range of activities or delivering things in a different order than your process usually requires, but this is happening for specific reasons that make sense now.

You have a choice, you can progress with the project and keep delivering more than what you signed off on, OR you renegotiate the terms of the deal.

As a consultant working closely with clients, you can often become an extension of their team. Therefore, it should be possible to open the door to a discussion where you lay out the challenge and invite your client to jointly resolve the issue. We got here together, so let's reshape this - together.

Again, I am reminded of our four-legged friend. While Wombats are very territorial, they choose to welcome others into their burrows, on their terms. During the 2020 bushfires that ravaged the East Coast of Australia, many animals were saved thanks to Wombats opening their homes to other creatures in danger. Their burrows can reach up to 30 metres deep, so must have provided an extraordinary sanctuary for animals under threat.

When you outline the situation, and the realities of what you're delivering versus what was anticipated, you can simply say – under these terms, 'This isn't working, so let's discuss how we move forward.'

By leading the discussion, you will not be left guessing as to whether they have an additional budget, or if they're open to rescoping the project altogether, or some other way forward.

Your power comes from being comfortable to forage for the answers, and not by scratching your head in your office frustrated by the way things are going, relative to the way you thought it would go. Instead, you will own these discussions, build your confidence and renegotiate your worth with ease.

WRAPPING IT UP

A group of WOMBATs is called a 'Wisdom". I have no doubt that you want to be part of that group.

Know your boundaries and ensure you mark your territory, by finding your voice and letting others know when what they're saying doesn't work for you.

Being comfortable saying no when you mean no isn't going to happen immediately. It's going to take practice, practice, and more practice – this will uncover 'your way' of saying no, so you're comfortable hearing the words come out of *your* mouth.

Commit to putting your needs on the same level as the clients you serve. Take stock and confirm each deal is a good deal for your business and your confidence.

All these steps will help you stay in the group – the 'Wisdom of WOMBATs'.

ACTION PLAN

What's the ONE action you'll take to harness your inner WOMBAT?

_____

FRILL-NECKED LIZARD

Finding BRAVERY within

This powerful yet small creature harnesses the characteristic of bravery. They do an incredible job of appearing larger than they are, especially when startled. They rise on their hind legs to let their incredibly colourful frill open to ensure predators don't underestimate them.

They are well known for their crazy running style, with many hours of YouTube video dedicated to hilarious voice over work.

Another cue we can take from 'Lizzie,' is how she sits quietly 'basking in the sun' for about 40 minutes every day, on a branch seemingly pondering, reflecting, and taking in the world around her. We too as business owners need to invest time in our 'basking,' reflecting and raising our awareness. Investing this time empowers us for when we're running around with arms and legs akimbo, successfully juggling all the balls we have in the air.

There are so many parallels between the mighty Frill-necked Lizard and being a business owner. From the day we start this pursuit, we want to appear larger than we actually are.

For example, I'm sure you've had the conversation about how you should write the 'About Us' page on your website – thinking, 'if I write 'WE' instead of 'ME', the business will appear bigger than just me.'

Once you do start to build a team around you, thinking back to this time seems so sweet, but the reality is wanting to appear bigger than you feel never really goes away, (well, I'm assuming, until you truly have a BIG business). It manifests in different ways, but it evolves as you grow.

Let's step through some of the ways you can unleash your inner Frill-necked Lizard powers.

BASKING ON THE DAILY

How many times have you been told 'You must spend more time working ON the business, instead of IN the business.' Gosh, that phrase has annoyed me so many times over the years. I know it makes good sense, but maybe it's just because I don't like rhetoric!

However, 'Lizzie' gives us a good look at how we could invest in ourselves each day by 'basking;' time well spent for all business owners. Not only because Vitamin D helps to keep bones, teeth and muscles healthy, but by investing in time to think means you can be agile, and ready to jump when opportunities present themselves. This time to reflect will also empower you and have a positive impact. Being aware of your brilliance and how your business is evolving will allow you to see where you need more focus.

MINDSET TIP

To help embrace this mindset idea, from the American spiritual teacher, psychologist, and author Ram Dass:

"The quieter you become, the more you can hear."

Throughout this book I have invited you to ponder your successes and your learnings. The purpose of YOUR Business Negotiator Toolkit is for you to capture your brilliance and to create your own language for use at future deals tables. Capturing your language, and your words and phrases, means it's personal to you, and having it handy means you will feel prepared and powerful when you're nervous about a deal. As well as many other power tools that will help you shine.

I've no doubt there are many other aspects of your role that would benefit from daily reflection. It's so important to pat yourself on the shoulder when you've done a good job; and to reflect on opportunities to grow, when things don't go to plan. However, we often kick ourselves and push harder and harder instead. Let's not do that!

If all else fails, run like a crazy person to the nearest tree like "Lizzie". Hopefully there is a resort somewhere nearby, so you can book yourself in for a week to rejuvenate.

FAKE IT 'TIL YOU MAKE IT

There are different times, circumstances, and deals that mean you'll be putting yourself forward for some big projects that you may be unsure you can handle. But if you don't do this, how will you grow.

It's a key to your success to feel confident, and sometimes that means you will have to fake it until you make it, by embracing situations that you're not sure you're ready for.

Taking risks such as putting yourself forward for bigger deals is similar to starting a job that may be out of your comfort zone – but if you don't go for it you'll just be vacillating, doing the easy stuff on repeat. That may be fun for a while as it's important to have a break from the pressure of always evolving, but as a person that uses their brain to make money, I'm pretty sure this won't hold your attention for too long.

There was a time, about three years into my business ownership journey, when I wasn't 100% fulfilled. The work I was doing was with great companies and people I liked working with however I wasn't jumping out of bed for it.

A wise mentor of mine made the observation that I was bored, that 'doing what I know how to do, is not what I've been programmed to do.' Prior to running my own show I'd had job after job, always stepping up into bigger roles I didn't fully know how to do. He said, 'See, it's time for you to give yourself a promotion.'

This blew my mind. It took so long to get the basics down that I hadn't even thought about being 'bored' in my own business. Alas, during my 'basking' after our discussion, I knew he was right. I needed to take some more risks, evolve the product mix and push into new, and bigger markets. This was SCCCCCAAAAAARRRRRRRYYYYYYY, as it meant I was playing a bigger game, against some brands MUCH bigger than mine but after unfurling my frills and standing on the tippy toes of my hind legs I started running towards these opportunities until the point where I knew I could do it, so I no longer needed the mask (for now).

I've no doubt, as I evolve, I will be embracing my inner 'Lizzie' many times over the years to come to ensure I appear bigger than I feel. Lizzie gives us a fabulous mask to embrace and step up with confidence.

BRAVERY FROM WITHIN

'Lizzie' has been an icon of power for a long time, depicted so wonderfully in the final scene of the classic cult film, The Adventures of Priscilla Queen of the Desert. The characters, two drag queens and a transgender woman, have been on a life-changing journey across outback Australia on a tour bus named 'Priscilla.' They've evolved as humans and friends; they've been through some tough times and had a lot of laughs.

In their final show, in a resort in Alice Springs, they perform a drag act to the song, Finally by CeCe Peniston, with wonderful Frill-necked Lizard costumes. They are so much more powerful and evolved as a result of the experiences they have encountered, which makes the scene unforgettable.

 To help you play your biggest game, take some time to capture the things that help you feel most powerful, in the *Power Tool 8: Know YOUR Power Indicators.*

WRAPPING IT UP

Similar to 'Lizzie', you are on an extraordinary adventure. Not every day is easy, but it is satisfying, and as you achieve milestones throughout the experience, there will be days where you may feel you have 'Finally' made it too.

Your bravado is replaced by true bravery when you know you can play a bigger game, because you believe in your powers, and you are able to back yourself at any deals table.

ACTION PLAN

What's the ONE action you'll take to harness your inner FRILL-NECKED LIZARD?

_____

YOUR BUSINESS NEGOTIATION TOOLKIT

This section is for you to make your very own Toolkit that will help transform your approach to negotiating your worth forever.

I truly believe everyone can become a good negotiator. By working your way through this book and filling out each of the sections, you'll feel closer to harnessing your powers from many different perspectives which will help you negotiate your worth with confidence.

Negotiating is a life skill, so the best results will come for you as you continue to build on what you've started. Take the actions you noted, practice what you learn, and continue to seek clarity on what you're capable of, so you can get great results at the deals table again and again.

Over time you'll find your new approach will become more natural, and just what you do as part of your negotiation process.

I encourage you to celebrate your successes along the way. Every bit of progress is important to take note of and enjoy. This will help you know how good you are, help you notice your progress, and make it obvious when you've 'done it' and love negotiating your worth.

You can also download these tools from our companion site:
negotiateyourworth.com.au/resources

WHAT'S INCLUDED IN YOUR BUSINESS NEGOTIATION TOOLKIT

YOUR ACTION PLAN

Throughout this book you've determined the actions you want to take to impact change and unleash your ability to become a powerful negotiator. You noted these at the end of each chapter. Now it's time to put them into action.

To make it easy for yourself to follow through on your actions, take a few minutes to flick back through the last page of each power animal. Transpose the action you noted at the end of each chapter into the table below, now add some more information about when you'll do it by and who can help you achieve it.

YOUR 8 POWER TOOLS

As there are 8 characteristics that make for a powerful negotiator, and they are represented by 8 power animals, there are 8 Power Tools that help guide you to Negotiate Your Worth.

MY NEGOTIATION FUNDAMENTALS

I have included a snapshot of the methodology I created in my first book, *I Love Negotiating*, which will complement all skills developed in this book, you can find this on pages 149 – 153.

POWER ANIMAL TO EMBRACE	HIDDEN POWER CHARACTERISTIC	POWER TOOL TO STRENGTHEN **YOUR** ABILITIES
Kookaburra	**PATIENTLY** unlocking the JOY	**YOUR** Negotiator Language Bank
Brushtail Possum	Identifying predictable **PATTERNS**	Behaviours of **YOUR** Ideal Client
Bilby	Harnessing your **RESILIENCE**	Identify **YOUR** Support Crew
Platypus	Being sensitive to enable **FLEXIBILTY**	Create **YOUR** rate card
Emu	Being boldy **CURIOUS**	Keep **YOUR** Curiosity in Negotiations
Red Kangaroo	**TRAILBLAZING** your path	When it's **YOUR** time to Turn Tail
Wombat	Being clear on **BOUNDARIES**	Articulate **YOUR** Boundaries
Frill-Necked Lizard	Finding **BRAVERY** within	Know **YOUR** Power Indicators

YOUR ACTION PLAN

It's time to put your plans into action.

To make it easy for yourself to follow through on your actions, take a few minutes to flick back through the last page of each power animal. Transpose the action you noted at the end of each chapter into the table below, now add some more information about when you'll do it by and who can help you achieve it.

Putting these actions into play is the key to your success, so ensure you set aside time in your diary to work through it, perhaps talk to your business coach about it too.

On the next page you'll find **YOUR Actions Plan** template, use this to collate all the actions you noted throughout the book. Also, to ensure they will get done, add time frames and the support you'll need, and lock in some time in your diary or with your business coach to work this through.

YOUR ACTION PLAN

POWER ANIMAL	POWER CHARACTERISTIC	ACTION I'LL TAKE...	WHEN I'LL DO IT BY...	WHO CAN HELP...
Kookaburra	**PATIENTLY** unlocking the JOY			
Brushtail Possum	Identifying predictable **PATTERNS**			
Bilby	Harnessing your **RESILIENCE**			
Platypus	Being sensitive to enable **FLEXIBILTY**			
Emu	Being boldy **CURIOUS**			
Red Kangaroo	**TRAILBLAZING** your path			
Wombat	Being clear on **BOUNDARIES**			
Frill-necked Lizard	Finding **BRAVERY** within			

POWER TOOL 1

KOOKABURRA – YOUR NEGOTIATOR LANGUAGE BANK

PATIENTLY unlocking the JOY

YOUR language will make you a powerful negotiator, this is better than any script I could write for you, so use this template to build YOUR bank of language, the language that works for you in negotiations.

Fill out this template as you work your way through this book, and into the future. It'll be your go-to guide on how you kick-butt in negotiations.

Look for the lessons when things don't go the way you planned. And when they do, ensure you capture the language that worked for you, noting down words, phrases, feelings, or anecdotes that will prepare you for future deals.

By identifying YOUR Negotiator Language, you can build on it every week until you start to get excited about negotiating your worth. It will begin to happen naturally and consistently work for you.

To start the process:

- Reflect on times **you've nailed a negotiation**. Be specific about the part of the discussion that went well and note it down below.

- Now, consider the ones that **didn't go as you'd hoped**. Again, be narrow about the part of the conversation that you can build on for next time.

This will become an ever-evolving reference tool of your negotiator brilliance. Continue building your language bank every time you engage in a negotiation that provides a lesson of note – capture them on the following pages:

POWER TOOL 1 » YOUR NEGOTIATOR LANGUAGE BANK

WHAT WAS THE SITUATION	LANGUAGE I USED (incl. body language)	HOW I FELT – DURING	HOW I FELT – ON REFLECTION	WHAT'S MY LESSON
e.g. Trying to close a deal that had been going on for a long time.	How close do you feel we are to reaching agreement?	Nervous to say it, but wanted to stop the back and forwards of this negotiation	Happy, because even though we didn't reach agreement, I could move on to something else.	I should ask questions like this earlier, when a deal is taking a long time to close.

POWER TOOL 1 » YOUR NEGOTIATOR LANGUAGE BANK - CONTINUED

WHAT WAS THE SITUATION	LANGUAGE I USED (incl. body language)	HOW I FELT – DURING	HOW I FELT – ON REFLECTION	WHAT'S MY LESSON
e.g. Trying to close a deal that had been going on for a long time.	How close do you feel we are to reaching agreement?	Nervous to say it, but wanted to stop the back and forwards of this negotiation	Happy, because even though we didn't reach agreement, I could move on to something else.	I should ask questions like this earlier, when a deal is taking a long time to close.

POWER TOOL 1 » YOUR NEGOTIATOR LANGUAGE BANK – CONTINUED

MY WATCH OUTS As you build **YOUR Negotiator Language Bank** you'll start to identify patterns of your own behaviour including any 'watch outs' you should be mindful of. These are things that you say, do or think when negotiating that may be helping your or hindering your success. Note these down increase your awareness and for you to consciously look for them:

MY BEHAVIOUR	MY ANTIDOTE
e.g. When I get frustrated, my cheeks go red	e.g. Be aware of heat in my face, and take a time out when it arises.

This tool is proof that you can be a powerful negotiator. By capturing your language you'll know what works for your, when you need it, and you'll never think, *"If only I had the right words"* – because you have them, here in **YOUR Negotiator Language Bank**.

POWER TOOL 2

BRUSHTAIL POSSUM – BEHAVIOURS OF YOUR IDEAL CLIENT

Identifying predictable **PATTERNS**

There are some clients that just don't fit with your business. They're looking for a different solution than you often, and value what you do very differently that you deserve.

They aren't bad, they just aren't your ideal client. To ensure you can negotiate your worth, it's imperative that you know who will value what you do (and who won't).

To help you with this, build out the behaviours of YOUR Ideal Client template.

POWER TOOL 2 » BEHAVIOURS OF YOUR IDEAL CLIENT

THINGS PEOPLE SAY THAT INDICATE THEY ARE YOUR IDEAL CLIENT ...
e.g. I really like that you have a methodology to support the roll out of this project.
• _____
• _____
• _____
• _____

POWER TOOL 2 » BEHAVIOURS OF YOUR IDEAL CLIENT

THINGS PEOPLE SAY THAT INDICATE THEY ARE NOT YOUR IDEAL CLIENT

e.g. 'Gosh you're expensive!

- _____
- _____
- _____
- _____
- _____

YOUR 'STANDARD' RESPONSE WHEN PEOPLE SAY THESE THINGS

Hmm, perhaps this isn't the right solution for you, what budget did you have in mind? (and how did you come up with that?)

- _____
- _____
- _____
- _____
- _____

POWER TOOL 3

BILBY – IDENTIFY YOUR SUPPORT CREW

Harnessing your **RESILIENCE**

One of the hardest challenges when running your own business is that you often feel like you're alone. However, it's possibly not as lonely as you think.

Consider all the people in your support crew, the people who work with you – your team, your accountant, suppliers, other business owners you collaborate with, or anyone in your network.

Then map them in the following table to ensure you're making the most of your team, so you go to the best person or people at the right time, so you remember, you're not alone, many people have got your back to help you succeed.

When faced with ongoing business challenges and negotiations you may just need someone to talk it through with. Help doesn't always need a skilled person; it may just need an objective perspective. So, reach out to your team and let them help you.

POWER TOOL 3 » IDENTIFY YOUR SUPPORT CREW

WHO'S MY GO-TO-PERSON

e.g. My mum

- _____
- _____
- _____
- _____
- _____

WHAT THEY'RE AWESOME AT...

Giving me perspective

- _____
- _____
- _____
- _____
- _____

POWER TOOL 3 » IDENTIFY YOUR SUPPORT CREW

WHAT THEY COULD HELP ME WITH...

Finding the calm, in a storm

- _____
- _____
- _____
- _____
- _____

HOW I KNOW I NEED TO TALK TO THEM...

When I'm facing an adversary at the deals table.

- _____
- _____
- _____
- _____
- _____

POWER TOOL 4

PLATYPUS – CREATE YOUR RATE CARD

Being sensitive to enable **FLEXIBILTY**

Having a rate card arms you with a measured response when potential clients want to know, 'how much do your services typically cost?'

If, instead, you don't know your numbers the whole process is set up for failure, with high levels of anxiety and stress.

Building a rate card will enable you to negotiate with confidence, because you'll know how you came up with the rates you charge and know where there is flexibility.

To help you do this, fill in the template on the following page:

You will likely evolve your products and aligned rates over time, so consider putting a note in your diary to review and update your rate card each year. That way you'll always be on the front foot when talking rates with clients.

POWER TOOL 4 » CREATE YOUR RATE CARD - PART 1

PRODUCT / SERVICE	WHAT EFFORT IS INVOLVED IN DELIVERY	WHAT ARE THE COSTS TO DELIVER IT	YOUR STANDARD RATES ARE...	SPECIAL RATES AND CONSIDERATIONS
e.g. End-to-end Strategy creation	Head hours, design, additional resources.	$xx, xxx	$xx, xxx, invoiced over xx months	e.g. 20% reduction for NFP clients

POWER TOOL 4 » CREATE YOUR RATE CARD - PART 2

INDUSTRY STANDARD RATES:	COMPARED TO COMPETITORS:	MY DIFFERENTIATORS:	RELATIVE TO A FULL-TIME SALARY RANGE:

POWER TOOL 5

EMU – KEEP YOUR CURIOSITY IN NEGOTIATIONS

Being boldy **CURIOUS**

Being a good negotiator is contingent on you being a good communicator, asking lots of questions and not shying away from key moments to ask them.

YOU CAN HANDLE 15 SECONDS OF PAIN

When you're sitting in a negotiation and are nervous about saying the price out loud to the client, instead of ignoring it and thinking, "I'll just email the quote through later". STOP. You've got this.

You just need to get the words from inside your head, past the (loud) beating of your nervous heart, and out of your mouth into the air. This can all be done with less than 15 seconds of pain.

You'll find the **PREPARE Cheat Sheet** as part of the **Negotiation Fundamentals** section on page 152.

POWER TOOL 5 » KEEP YOUR CURIOSITY IN NEGOTIATIONS

HESITATING IN A NEGOTIATION, ASK YOURSELF:

» **WHAT'S THE WORST THING THAT COULD HAPPEN?**

» **WHAT'S THE BEST THING THAT COULD HAPPEN?**

» **WHAT I'LL SAY NEXT...**

**Then, once you've *said it out loud*,
DON'T say anything for 15 seconds...**

Shhhh.

Wait for them to process what you've said, ponder it, then respond.

The awkward 15 seconds where you're waiting for them to respond but dying to jump in and fill the silence. It hurts for such a very short amount of time, but this will help you become stronger and bolder at every deals table.

WHEN SHOULD I TALK TO CLIENTS ABOUT MONEY?

ANY TIME YOU CAN!

BUT, do NOT negotiate over email.

This infographic is a reminder of ways to help you stay curious when you're negotiating, put it on your wall so you see it every day.

AM I ALLOWED TO ASK THAT – HECK YES!!

Whenever you're holding back from asking a question in a negotiation, just ask it.

Write it on your notepad first, then ask it.

You're the boss, if you don't ask it, who will?

POWER TOOL 6

BIG RED KANGAROO – WHEN IT'S YOUR TIME TO TURN TAIL

TRAILBLAZING your path

Knowing when to turn tail needs to be mastered to clear paths and provide the freedom to Trailblaze.

Use this checklist to help you identify when you need to make a big call and say 'thanks, but no thanks' to a client.

POWER TOOL 6 » WHEN IT'S YOUR TIME TO TURN TAIL

QUESTION TO EXPLORE MY POSITION	YES	NO
Are they talking like my ideal client?		
Is my gut saying I'm going to enjoy working with this client?		
Does it feel like this is a fair exchange in value?		
Is this project the type of work I want to be doing?		
Does this deal make good economic sense for my business?		
When talking with this client, does it feel easy?		
MY DETERMINATION:	STAY	GO

IF I DECIDE IT'S TIME TO TURN TAIL, I COULD SAY...
e.g. Thanks for the opportunity, I'm not sure we're the best team to deliver this. If it helps, I could introduce you to xxx, who is better suited to this type of work/budget.

- _____

- _____

There may be a number of situations that require different responses to help you exit a deal. By capturing these responses over time will ensure that you have the words your need to manage an uncomfortable conversation with ease.

POWER TOOL 7

WOMBAT – ARTICULATING YOUR MESSAGE

Being clear on your **BOUNDARIES**

Being clear on your boundaries and how to articulate them to others has a significant impact on your success in negotiations. Use this tool as a way to capture how you'll do this with others.

5 Ways to say 'NO' like a BOSS:

- No, BUT...
- No, THANK YOU...
- No, AND...
- No, MAYBE...
- NO.

POWER TOOL 7 » ARTICULATING YOUR MESSAGE

ADDITIONAL WAYS I SAY 'NO' ...
• _____
• _____
• _____
• _____
• _____

POWER TOOL 7 » ARTICULATING YOUR MESSAGE

LANGUAGE CHOICE

To ensure I'm comfortable during emotionally charged negotiations I use these words to depersonalise the conversation:

- Replace 'you' with 'the company'.

- Swap 'me' with 'someone in my position'

- Change 'I believe' with 'a reasonable person would think/do/act'

ADDITIONAL LANGUAGE I CHOOSE INCLUDES: ...

- _____

- _____

- _____

- _____

- _____

- _____

- _____

- _____

Building your bank of ways to articulate where your boundaries are, and where you draw the line, will ensure you're clear on what they actually are and how you'll share them with others.

POWER TOOL 8

FRILL NECKED-LIZARD – KNOW YOUR POWER INDICATORS

Finding **BRAVERY** within

Taking time for yourself is a key part of your survival and comfort to secure great outcomes for your business. To do this everyone is different, so take some time to note down the things you need to feel most powerful:

POWER TOOL 8 » KNOW YOUR POWER INDICATORS

THE ACTIVITIES THAT HELP ME FEEL POWERFUL ARE:
e.g. Taking time to prepare for every negotiation, so I feel powerful as I approach the conversation.
• _____
• _____
• _____
• _____

POWER TOOL 8 » KNOW YOUR POWER INDICATORS

THE PEOPLE THAT HELP ME FEEL POWERFUL ARE:

e.g. Spending time with xxx from my support crew to talk about any big deals I'm facing.

- _____
- _____
- _____
- _____

THE MINDSET THAT HELPS ME FEEL MOST POWERFUL IS:

e.g. Ensuring I have a growth mindset when approaching a challenging negotiation. Breaking it down into components to focus on helps me with this.

- _____
- _____
- _____

Pondering what you need in order to play a big game regularly will help you have the energy to negotiate outstanding outcomes for your business, so ensure you invest time in building this power tool.

MY NEGOTIATION FUNDAMENTALS

To ensure you're set up for success these negotiation fundamentals, which are established in my book "I Love Negotiating", will guide your approach.

1. SHIFT YOUR LANGUAGE

Stop referring to them as negotiations. Refer to them as *conversations*, or a series of conversations.

2. NEGOTIATING ISN'T A FIGHT

Don't shy away from a negotiation because you think it's going to be a fight. Healthy debate is one thing but arguing isn't negotiating.

3. DAMN THE TABOOS – EMBRACE UNCOMFORTABLE CONVERSATIONS

Negotiating great outcomes in business means we need to acknowledge and ignore many cultural taboos. Every day, you...

- have to talk about money, despite it being considered rude to do so.
- need to say what you want, even though people say that means you're being pushy,

- should tell people what you don't want, and you aren't being difficult by doing so, and
- must articulate your worth with people you don't know, you're not bragging you're helping them understand why you're worth every cent based on your past success.

4. THE GOAL OF GOOD NEGOTIATIONS

A good negotiation finishes with **a fair and reasonable exchange of value**.

This approach invites you to start a dialogue: Is what I'm asking for fair? Is what I want in exchange reasonable? This will help you determine if this a good deal for you, or if you should walk away.

5. APEC FRAMEWORK: THE FOUR STAGES OF A GOOD NEGOTIATION

To help you achieve your goal in a negotiation, you need a process. My APEC Framework can help guide you through the four stages of a good negotiation. By consistently working your way through this simple, yet effective process, you'll feel more confident.

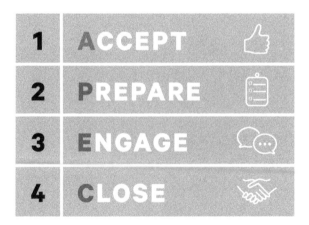

- The first stage is to **ACCEPT** that this is happening. Decide to actively become involved in (more) negotiations or in a particular negotiation you may have been avoiding.

- To enhance your chance of success, you must **PREPARE**. Invest the bulk of you time in this stage – I suggest as much as 70% of your time to clarify your thinking. Use this time to know where you're willing to be flexible, to conduct research, test your positioning, and create your PREPARE Cheat Sheet (outlined below).

- As you **ENGAGE** in the negotiation, armed with your PREPARE Cheat Sheet, you're ready to present your case, being mindful of possible roadblocks, and steering the conversation toward achieving your goal.

- In the final stages of a negotiation, it's time to **CLOSE**. Secure the best deal or walk away, ensuring you leave with no ambiguity around the outcome.

If you want to explore this in more detail, visit the site **www.negotiateyourworth. com.au/resources** for more content, or read my first book, I Love Negotiating.

6. A BALANCED APPROACH

Regardless of if you are the type of person who likes to WING IT or CHOREOGRAPH IT when it comes to key conversations, I recommend you flip your approach when it comes to negotiations.

Instead, consciously take a balanced approach so you are **well prepared with flexibility built in**. This will help you think clearly, be creative and enter the room with confidence.

7. YOUR PREPARE CHEAT-SHEET

Your PREPARE Cheat Sheet is a one-page summary that guides your preparation for each negotiation. You will fill it out, test it and take it into your negotiations.

It guides your focus, helping you get clear on what you want; when you'll walk away; what the supporting points for your case are; and other notes to help you confidently participate in the negotiation.

APEC PREPARE CHEATSHEET

This tool will help guide the PREPARE stage of your negotiations, time and time again.

ACCEPT

PREPARE

4 stages
to good
negotiations

ENGAGE

CLOSE

The focus of this negotiation is...

The meeting invitation will read:

What I want to achieve is...

Why I feel entitled to this (in one sentence)...

Why now is the right time to ask for this...

My supporting points of evidence are...

☐

☐

☐

☐

My counter-discussion points are...

☐ If they say this ....

☐ I'll say this ....

☐ If they say this ....

☐ I'll say this ....

What I'm asking for is...

Dream outcome..............................

Ideal outcome................................

Walk away ....

What else could be in the deal:.

My personal watch-outs...

The antidote is...

Who I'll talk this through with...

Who: What they are likely to bring:

Next steps - actions, owner, timing:

These fundamentals should put you in a healthy mindset towards negotiating. Clarity on the aim and knowing there is a methodology to guide you will hold you in good stead as you approach the deals table.

But the key to your success is to implement change, just like learning a new language or a musical instrument, you have to practice. Neuroscientists say the best way to make new neural pathways (patterns) is through repetition and practice, that way, those connections will be established enough to become habitual or default behaviours.

Once you've learnt to embrace your brilliance in negotiating, it will have a positive impact throughout many aspects of your life.

It will change the way you look at personal negotiations, help you approach uncomfortable conversations more directly and push aside taboos that don't serve you.

You can start to embrace opportunities to secure a fair and reasonable exchange of the value you bring to the table for clients.

Over time you'll even start to enjoy yourself at the deals table, because you'll be able to negotiate your worth with ease.

Good luck!

CLOSE

Well, that's it! That's how I recommend you embrace your ability to approach the deals table with confidence to negotiate your worth.

You CAN achieve success on a regular basis. You simply need to be kind to yourself. Work through the actions you've set for yourself through the pages of this book. Though this may feel like heavy lifting, the upside will be worth it as it will pay long-term dividends.

I know you CAN become a good negotiator. Look around at all the times you do it well and embrace the hidden powers of our furry friends for the parts you are working on.

Every business owner is given the gift of eternal evolution. The ability to try new things, build products with whoever you like, and work with people who respect your abilities, while also regularly shifting the goal posts.

I found this so liberating, but I appreciate it also comes with challenges. There will be times where you get it wrong, for when you short-change yourself in a deal. Don't beat yourself up, go through the process, dissect where it went well and where it could have gone better, and implement change the next time around, allowing you to grow and your confidence to bounce back.

I hope that by working your way through this book, you now have clarity on your value and what you deliver to clients. I am confident that you CAN negotiate great deals for your business, and you are comfortable to walk away from deals that don't work for you.

MEASURING HOW FAR YOU'VE COME

Early in this book you completed **YOUR Negotiator Strengths Self-Assessment** to rate yourself on how you negotiated before you started this journey with me, pondering a time you have nailed a negotiation, and parts of negotiating that make you uncomfortable and those that you don't think twice about.

Take a look over the responses you noted back then, perhaps ask yourself those same questions again now.

What's shifted? Where can you now identify yourself as a powerful negotiator?

Having this as a reference point to see how far you've come; you can review it every time you pick up this book. Each time you work through it you'll see even more progress.

TOP TAKEAWAYS

POWER ANIMAL	TOP TAKE AWAY
Kookaburra	Learning patience, investing in observing, and listening with intent will help you find the joy in the negotiation process.
Brushtail Possum	Identify predictable behaviours in the people you do and don't want to work with will reduce the amount of stress, anxiety and uncertainty you experience in every negotiation.
Bilby	Harnessing your resilience, keeping your options open and realising 'you're not alone in this', will improve your ability to enjoy the roller-coaster you've jumped on, as well as seeing your business flourish through adverse times.
Platypus	Being clear on how you came up with your rates, enables you to determine when you're willing to be flexible, based on environmental sensitivities.
Emu	Ambiguity spells the death of many potential deals - if instead you're boldly curious, and don't shy away from opportunities to ask good questions you'll stand tall and push forward with great power.
Red Kangaroo	Forging your own path isn't always easy, as the boss you must do what it takes to survive, meaning you have to confidently walk away from deals you know aren't right for you.
Wombat	Setting your boundaries and knowing your no-go areas gives you strength to secure great outcomes at the deals table.
Frill-necked Lizard	Investing time to reflect and identify ways to play a bigger game will set you up well to bravely embrace wherever each crazy day may take you.

MORAL OF THE STORY

I hope you found joy in the use of the metaphors in our nation's extraordinarily, unique and powerful native animals. I wanted to make the process of building your negotiation capability FUN, so I hope you had a giggle from time to time, and it made it easier for you to learn the lessons I'm sharing.

I will always LOVE Negotiating, and I have NO doubt that if you've worked your way through the book to this point, you probably do too (now).

I hope, by completing this book, you find yourself stepping up to the deals table with more of a spring in your step, having become empowered and confident – because you're worth a great deal.

MY LEARNINGS FROM WRITING

Writing this book has been a big experience for me. At times it has been painful, making myself remember the challenges I've encountered as an 'accidental business owner,' and the numerous rounds of testing and learning at the deals table, reviewing where it did or did not go well, and the impact it had on my confidence.

There were some really tough days and weeks I had to remember through this process; times where, if it wasn't for my support network, and my grit, I would have chucked it all in and got a job. That was painful to relive.

BUT I am so thankful for the experience. Every year I get to throw spaghetti at the wall to see what sticks. Every day I get to live my life by design and work with people I like, doing stuff I love, like writing this book. And I appreciate that so much.

This freedom has provided me the opportunity to take an honest look at the patterns in my experiences that I have summarised to share with you.

WHERE TO FROM HERE

I hope you have derived a lot of value by working through Negotiate Your Worth.

You may be wondering, 'Where to from here?', to continue to grow your negotiation capability. There are a number of options available for this:

VISIT THE BOOK WEBSITE

negotiateyourworth.com.au This is where you'll find additional content, information about the other products we offer as an extension of the content in these pages. And, remember, you can also download the templates from YOUR Business Negotiator Toolkit from this site.

WORK WITH THE AUTHOR (and her team)

If you'd like some additional support in transforming the way you approach negotiating to secure great outcomes for yourself and your business, reach out to the Other Side of the Table team.

We help you make the most of every deal you invest in.
Behind every successful deal is a sound strategy and a confident negotiator with the ability to secure a **fair and reasonable exchange in value**.

Because it's worth a great deal.

There are 3 pillars to our business:
CAPABILITY BUILDING – Empowering your team to negotiate better outcomes with ease.

STRATEGIC GROWTH – Exploring every possibility to develop a strategic approach to help you achieve your goals.

ADVOCATING CHANGE – Changing the way Australian's think, feel and approach negotiating.

Our team's way

With a practical approach to everything we do, our tools, strategic frameworks and expert advice are delivered to make an enduring impact.

We empower you and your team to negotiate better outcomes with ease. We love negotiating and have a passion for bringing a strategic approach to every deal's table - and we're on a mission to help you love it too!

The Other Side of the Table team supports you to make the most of every deal you invest in. Helping you navigate the highs and lows of the negotiation process, shifting your mindset, and empowering you to consistently negotiate great outcomes with confidence, in all situations.

To find out more by visiting **www.othersideofthetable.com.au** OR get in touch with us at **support@othersideofthetable.com.au**

ABOUT THE ARTIST

JILL BARBER RICHARDSON, PAINTER AND OTHER STUFF

Artist Jill Barber Richardson was born in the same town as Waltzing Matilda nine months after a 100 year flood. It's fair to say the bush has influenced her from an early age. Raised on a sheep and cattle station in Central Western Queensland, Jill completed her primary schooling by correspondence.

As a teenager her artistic talents were quickly recognised and nurtured while at boarding school and later she was accepted at the Queensland College of Art but decided to explore her love of science and agriculture instead and put her art aspirations to the side.

The third of four daughters, family and animals were always the centre of Jill's early life. Like most childhoods spent in the bush, hers was one filled many joys as well as the lows of drought and flood. Over the years there have been many special pets, horses and poddy sheep and calves that have touched her life and influenced her depiction of animals.

In every portrait there is the soul of one of those animals. Capturing the personality of a much loved pet, a noble horse, a wise old cow, is a much more than drawing on a page. It is a rare talent to capture a kind eye, a tired body, a wise old face of salt and pepper on black muzzle. It is an exceptional skill that Jill Richardson has made her own.

Jill and her husband Richo currently reside in western Victoria on their family sheep and cropping farm with their four children. She is still surrounded and inspired by the animals she loves.

Sam and Jill met at that boarding school, so creating the artwork for Sam's book was an exciting and warmly received invitation to collaborate. Jill has a strong connection with her childhood friendships and honours them with the upmost importance.

Jill was thrilled to be part of this project, that recognised her ability to illustrate the emotions and characteristics animals show.

Artwork and more...

If you'd like to support an Australian artist, you can purchase Jill's artwork, commission a piece or even grab a handbag from:
www.jillbarberrichardson.com
instagram: jillbarberrichardsonart

TARONGA PARTNERSHIP

TARONGA
CONSERVATION SOCIETY
AUSTRALIA.

As animals play such a significant role in this book, we forged a partnership with the Taronga Conservation Society Australia.

Taronga is a not-for-profit organisation and everything they do is for the wild.

$1 from the sale of each copy of Negotiate Your Worth will be donated and these funds will go directly back into the support, care and conservation of wildlife.

Taronga believes that wildlife and people can share this planet and that all of us have a responsibility to protect the world's precious wildlife, not just in our lifetimes, but for the generations of the future.

Through their clear vision to help secure a shared future for wildlife and people, Taronga engages in activities that span the fields of animal care, recovery, education, community engagement, guest experience and science.

Taronga is a world-renowned conservation organisation operating two Zoos in New South Wales. At Taronga Zoo in Sydney and Taronga Western Plains Zoo in Dubbo, they lead conservation efforts in the field and participate in regional and global conservation breeding programs to establish insurance populations for species threatened in the wild.

Across their two sites, Taronga operates two wildlife hospitals that treat and rehabilitate injured native wildlife, as well as providing best practice health care for the animals at their Zoos. Through Taronga's breed for release programs and the rehabilitation of animals at their wildlife hospitals, Taronga has released over 50,000 animals to the wild.

To provide further support to Taronga and learn more about their mission, please visit **taronga.org.au**

APPRECIATION AND PRIASE

When setting out to write my second book I thought I had some idea of how it might play out. However, the twists and turns it took in form and function throughout the process was very surprising.

The first words were written in the Smokey Mountains, Tennessee while sharing an experience of a lifetime with my sister, Shanny. And I wrote the final words on Norfolk Island while taking a mini-break during a global pandemic.

I've shared this experience with many people, and I even managed to write more than one book while writing this one. The elements of the book that were pulled out will appear in a collaboration with some amazing people when we get to Spaghetti on the Wall.

None of this would have been possible without the guidance and patience of Diane Hopkins my incredibly talented and patient Book Coach. The iterations, highs and lows of the writing experience were a shared one, thank you Diane.

To my work family – Sarah Procajlo, Stacey Packer (the one who has read every word on every line, multiple times - you are amazing, thank you), Isobel Darmody, Nicole Hatherley, Margot Andersen and my other 'support crew' members – you make working for myself fun, challenging, different and exciting, who could ask for more, thank you!

For the support and feedback on the early drafts, thank you for your generosity and honesty Jade Collins (from Femeconomy) and my friend Luke Maquire – it did make me happy when you told me not to throw it in the bin, thank you.

To my incredible friends and family who have listened to me ~~rabbit~~, I mean Bilby, on about this book for a long while. I appreciate you always being there to bounce ideas off, laughing off the silly perspectives and drowning out the dumb ones. Special thanks to my brutally honest besties – Keith Jones and Brendan McGovern, thanks for your sledge hammer honesty and endless abilities to make me laugh at myself and life – here's to Nachos, Rocket and Caesar for bringing us together.

To the team at KMD Books, especially Karen McDermott, thank you.

To Jill Barber Richardson, the incredibly talented artist that has brought such beauty and creativity to support the words in this book. I had a clear image of what I wanted the artwork to be like, but you took that and smashed it out of the park. I've loved your artwork since we were at school, and I'm so proud to have these magical pieces of your art to cherish forever. Thank you, thank you, thank you (and I promise I'll never ask you to create another lizard).

Thank you to my friends at Taronga Zoo for your guidance and interest in this project, especially Nick Boyle and Suzy Scheiblin. Thank you, Jill and I are grateful for your enthusiasm and invaluable feedback about the copy, context and artwork. Here's to supporting the conservation of our incredible Australian natives for a long time to come!

To all my clients, past, present and future – I appreciate the opportunity to learn through our shared experiences and problem solving, ensuring every day is different, thank you for the trust and the opportunities to hone my craft to be able to share it with others.

Thank you.

Printed in Australia
AUHW010748080322
360589AU00001B/1